Graphis Mission Statement: Graphis is commited to presenting exceptional work in international design, advertising, illustration and photography. Since 1944 we have presented individuals and companies in the visual communications industry who have consistently demonstrated excellence and determination in overcoming economic, cultural and creative hurdles to produce brilliance.

Advertising Annual 2003

The International Annual of Advertising
Das internationale Jahrbuch der Plakakunst
Le répertoire internationale de l'art de l'affiche

CEO & Creative Director: B. Martin Pedersen

Editor: Michael Porciello

Art Director: Lauren Prigozen
Design & Production: Nicole Recchia
Luis Diaz, Alexia Leitich, and Joanne Sullivan

Published by Graphis Inc.

This book is dedicated to
Jay Chiat

(opposite) 'Airplane' ad for Corlison Pte. Ltd. by Impiric Singapore, page 130.

Contents Inhalt Sommaire

Remarks: We extend our heartfelt thanks to contributors throughout the world who have made it possible to publish a wide and international spectrum of the best work in this field. Entry instructions for all Graphis Books may be requested from: **Graphis Inc.**, 307 Fifth Avenue, Tenth Floor, New York, NY 10016, or visit our Web site at www.graphis.com. *Anmerkungen:* Unser Dank gilt den Einsendern aus aller Welt, die es uns ermöglicht haben, ein breites, internationales Spektrum der besten Arbeiten zu veröffentlichen. Teilnahmebedingungen für die Graphis-Bücher sind erhältlich bei: **Graphis Inc.**, 307 Fifth Avenue, Tenth Floor, New York, NY 10016. Besuchen Sie uns im World Wide Web, www.graphis.com. *Remerciements:* Nous remercions les participants du monde entier qui ont rendu possible la publication de cet ouvrage offrant un panorama complet des meilleurs travaux. Les modalités d'inscription peuvent être obtenues auprès de: **Graphis Inc.**, 307 Fifth Avenue, Tenth Floor, New York, NY 10016. Rendez-nous visite sur notre site web: www.graphis.com. © Copyright under universal copyright convention copyright © 2002 by Graphis Inc., 307 Fifth Avenue, Tenth Floor, New York, NY 10016. Jacket and book design copyright © 2002 by Graphis, Inc. No part of this book may be reproduced in any form without written permission of the publisher. ISBN: 1-931241-14-7 Printed in Hong Kong. Distributed in North America by Publishers Group West. Distributed in all other countries by HBI/HarperCollins.

(opposite) 'Ice Princess' ad for Duncan Hines by Bozell New York, page 105.

JAY CHIAT
(1931-2002)

Jay Chiat, a giant in the world of advertising, died at his home in Marina Del Rey, California, on April 23 2002, after a long battle with prostate cancer. He was 70 years old.☐Chiat, who will be remembered as having revolutionized advertising in the '70s and '80s, was perhaps best known for the "1984" spot that launched Apple's Macintosh computer during Super Bowl XVIII. The $1 million ad, directed by Ridley Scott, cast Big Blue as Big Brother in an Orwellian nightmare of office drones. Considered the most successful commercial ever, it was shown on national television only once, but set the standard for the ad frenzy that has come to mark the Super Bowl and forever set Apple apart from its competitors.☐Born Morton Jay Chiat in New York City on October 25, 1931, Chiat graduated from Rutgers University in 1953. After serving as a public information officer in the Air Force, he worked on recruitment advertising for the military contractor Aerojet General.☐In 1956, he moved to Orange County, California and began work as a copywriter at Leland Oliver Co. In 1962 he opened Jay Chiat & Associates. Six years later the shop merged with Faust/Day. From the start Chiat/Day developed a reputation for breaking the conventions of the industry by creating irreverent ads infused with references to popular culture. During the 1984 Summer Olympics, Chiat/Day pushed Nike shoes with a campaign featuring Randy Newman's "I Love L.A.," and buildings converted into giant billboards with portraits of towering atheletes. In 1989 the agency debuted the tireless Energizer Bunny for Eveready.☐By the early '90s, Chiat/Day was an international agency with 1,200 employees and $1.3 billion in billings. It was named "Agency of the Decade" by Advertising Age magazine, after earning the title "Agency of the Year" in 1980 and 1988.☐In 1993, Chiat gave the world its first "virtual office," replacing his employees' cubicles and offices with portable phones and computers, shared tables and lockers. The experiment was housed in Chiat/Day's Venice, California, headquarters, through collaboration between architect Frank Gehry and the sculptors Claes Oldenburg and Coosje van Bruggen in the form of a four-story pair of field glasses. It was later continued in a New York office designed by Gaetano Pesce. Though hailed as visionary by the press, Chiat's employees considered it a failure.☐In 1995 Chiat/Day was sold to Omnicom Group. After a three-year break, Jay Chiat became chairman of Screaming Media, a Manhattan-based Internet content distributor to such major clients as America Online, Sun Microsystems and Microsoft.☐The American Advertising Federation made him a member of its Hall of Fame in March 1999. The Rutgers University Alumni Federation named him to its Hall of Distinguished Alumni in 2000. At the induction ceremony, Chiat, who'd been instrumental in helping minorities in the field of advertising, pledged $1 million to Rutgers to create a scholarship program for disadvantaged African-American and Latino students.☐This book is dedicated to the memory of Jay Chiat.

IS IT LOVE?

For further information please visit us at MINI.com or call +49 (0)800 123 456 (€ 0.12/minute)

20 Questions on Advertising by Warren Berger

20 Questions on Advertising by Warren Berger

Do you consider advertising to be an art, a science—or both? (If both, does it lean more one way than the other?)
Advertising is not art. Art is creativity without any logos stuck on it.

Cite an example of one of the best ads you've ever created; What makes it a good ad?
MINI Cooper—"Interior." It's simple. It doesn't try too hard. It makes you smile. (Hopefully.)

How do you set up an agency environment that fosters creativity?
We try to create a relaxed atmosphere in our agency. A few examples: Every morning the staff gets fresh fruit, cheese, bread and other nice things from the market and we have break-fast together. After that, we en-courage people to work outside the agency away from the phones and the account guys. (I usually sit half a day in a cafe around the corner thinking about ideas.) Instead of sending people to Cannes, we send them to film festivals at Sundance and Ams-terdam. And after working for three years at Jung von Matt you get two months off to relax and refresh your mind.

How important is research/planning in creating great ads?
Planning is like a pass in football: If it's a good one, it helps us put the ball in the net. If it's bad, Brazil wins again.

How much should one rely on intuition and gut instinct?
I rely on my gut instinct only when I try to come up with an idea. I try to feel what's right to do for the product or the brand. I don't research very much. I just look at the product and it's almost like the product talks to me. It tells me about its character, what it has to say and what's special about it. I'm writing down those things and somehow they turn into a campaign. But I still don't know how exactly that last part works. It just happens somehow.

What inspires you?
Feature films and running. At the moment I am into John Cassavetes. A lot of ideas come to me when I am on a long distance run.

Is it possible to both manage creative people and also create your own work?
I usually have all my meetings in the morning: I see the teams, speak to clients on the phone and do what's there to be done. For lunch I go out and stay out until the evening to think about ideas.

Do you think advertising creators have a responsibility to the public?
We all are educated by the stuff that surrounds us. And advertising has a big part in that. If it's dull, people get duller. If it is funny, people are a little happier. If it's interesting or if it tells people something new... that's the best.

In your opinion, do clients trust ad agencies as much as they should?
If all agencies always did good work, clients would trust us. But there is so much crap on TV, which makes the clients think:

"Ads mainly stink. So I better watch out what my agency does!" And I can understand that. Trust comes after a couple of years of good ads.

What is the most unusual form you've seen an ad take (i.e. side-walk ads, etc.)? Do you think it was effective?
MINI Cooper S—"Locomo-tion." The media you can't buy from a media agency is the most effective: It's already creative to find that new place where you can surprise somebody.

Which ad or campaign (by someone else) do you most admire?
The Volkswagen campaign. The English and the American one.

Is there any subject or source material (politics, the Bible, the Beatles) that should be off-limits to advertisers?
No. No taboos.

Is controversy a good thing for some advertisers?
I just don't like ads that are trying too hard to be shocking. Otherwise I love controversy. It's gets you thinking.

Do you think the West–particularly the US and UK–sets the pace for the rest of the world in advertising, or have other regions now taken the lead?
I have always loved Asia. They probably have the same difficulties as the Germans: Most of their ads only make sense within their own culture. But I love their art direction, their photography and design.

Will advertising continue to merge & blend with entertain-ment content, and is that a good thing for the audience?
I hate being interrupted by an ad while I watch a film on TV. I really hate it. No matter how good the ads are. I think ads should let the audience decide if they want to look at it or not.

Who was your past mentor/inspiration in advertising?
Filmmakers like Scorsese, Lynch, Truffaut, Polanski, Kazan, Kieslowski.

Who do you most admire in your profession today?
I like a lot of people in advertising. But mainly because they are nice people, not just because they had good ideas.

If an ad is well-liked by the public and wins awards, yet the product does not sell as a result, what (if anything) can we conclude from that?
The audience and the creatives still had fun.

What will spark the next "Creative Revolution" in advertising?
Media neutral.

Over to you—any final thoughts on advertising?
I never know where ideas come from. I just know that it's great to have one. So I am on my way to the café now.

Oliver Voss became Creative Managing Director at Jung von Matt/Alster in Hamburg, after tenures at Deutsch Advertising in New York and Wieden + Kennedy, Amsterdam.

(opposite and opening page) Creativity with logos stuck on it, by Jung von Matt

Do you consider advertising to be an art, a science—or both? (If both, does it lean more one way than the other?)
The best advertising has some art to the science and usually has science behind the art.

Cite an example of one of the best ads you've ever created; What makes it a good ad?
The hippo ad for Polaris Watercraft. Stopping power visually. And a relevant point of view in copy.

How do you set up an agency environment that fosters creativity?
(no comment)

How important is research/planning in creating great ads?
If you can afford it, use it. It's the ammunition for creating great work.

How much should one rely on intuition and gut instinct?
Depends on the level of understanding the creative person has of their target.

What inspires you?
Creative minds with good atti-

tudes. My children. My wife. Music.

Is it possible to both manage creative people and also create your own work?
It is, but it's hard. The more accounts you have the less you should do work. You need perspective when you're managing. That's hard when also making the work.

Do you think advertising creators have a responsibility to the public?
Yes.

In your opinion, do clients trust ad agencies as much as they should?
No.

What is the most unusual form you've seen an ad take (i.e. sidewalk ads, etc.)? Do you think it was effective?
(no comment)

Which ad or campaign (by someone else) do you most admire?
(no comment)

Is there any subject or source material (politics, the Bible, the

Beatles) that should be off-limits to advertisers?
The only limitation I would pose is if it serves no purpose other than to hurt people.

Is controversy a good thing for some advertisers?
Yes, if it aids in recall.

Do you think the West—particularly the US and UK—sets the pace for the rest of the world in advertising, or have other regions now taken the lead?
(no comment)

Will advertising continue to merge & blend with entertainment content—and is that a good thing for the audience?
Yes. It's good only if the audience wants it.

Who was your past mentor/inspiration in advertising?
Too many to mention.

Who do you most admire in your profession today?
The ones down the hall from me.

If an ad is well-liked by the public and wins awards, yet the product does not sell as a result, what (if anything) can we con-

clude from that?
There's so much more to selling a product then just the ad. I can't conclude until I understand all aspects of the situation. Marketing mix, Product reliability, Distribution, etc.

What will spark the next "Creative Revolution" in advertising?
Britney Spears.

Over to you—any final thoughts on advertising?
I like it. It's cool.

Brian Kroening is a Group Creative Director and Senior Partner at Carmichael Lynch. He has contributed to campaigns for Lawson Software, Gibson Guitars, the American Advertising Federation, Brown Forman Wines, American Standard, Formica and Hurd Windows. An accomplished songwriter and musician, Brian has two CD's on the shelves at Best Buy. When not hanging out with wife Lisa, pre-schooler Samuel and baby Nicholas, Brian still performs his music as time permits (yeah right).

(opposite) Ads for Cross pens by Carmichael Lynch

Do you consider advertising to be an art, a science—or both? (If both, does it lean more one way than the other?)
Neither an art nor a science. For me, advertising is a set of communication- and commercial persuasion techniques combined with some sense of entertainment. Unfortunately, half of the advertising creators think advertising is merely a collection of odd, funny ads. The other half see it as a boring exercise intended to show the physical characteristics of products and their prices. Advertising is only good when it is able to attract and hold the audience's attention to the real benefits of brands and products in an interesting and seductive way.

Cite an example of one of the best ads you've ever created; What makes it a good ad?
Some years ago, I created an ad for a publisher that wanted to promote the habit of reading real books instead of reading them through computers. It's quite a simple ad, but I love it. It is about something that touches everybody and uses text and images that synthesize what could happen if books disappeared. The photo in the ad shows a man sitting on a toilet with a computer in his lap. The picture stresses the inconvenience and ridiculousness of such a situation. It is an objective example of what I consider to be the objective of advertising: To inform and entertain at the same time.

How do you set up an agency environment that fosters creativity?
You need to set up an environment that combines relaxation and responsibility. Relaxation because working in advertising is already stressful enough; the agency environment shouldn't make things worse. Responsibility because you have to build some walls so as to avoid work becoming total madness without any sort of commitment regarding deadlines, budgets and lines of communication with the customer. At Edson, FCB, we've developed a layout with no individual rooms or desks. All of the staff in the agency—about 70 people—sit at six tables distributed in a way that resembles a ring-shaped donut. There are only two hierarchies. Everyone in the agency is involved in the creation and development of adver-

tising projects every day, which has eliminated that bad atmosphere of typical advertising agencies.

How important is research/planning in creating great ads?
I believe advertising is an interactive activity: those who create it must keep their eyes and ears wide open to the customers' habits and customs. But I don't stand up for the abusive use of research. Most heavily research-based ads turn out to be cold ads that fail to motivate the viewer. The customer mustn't take the place of the advertiser in their task of creating ads.

How much should one rely on intuition and gut instinct?
Not much. Instinct is good, but it doesn't solve everything. Being methodical and having the capacity to gather and synthesize information are all part of the advertiser's job.

What inspires you?
Life

Is it possible to both manage creative people and also create your own work?
That's my daily job. Sometimes it's a maddening task: the nature of creative work demands a certain space of liberty to create. But while managing creatives you realize how much time you waste developing paths that are absolutely wrong and impracticable. So, when you are going to create, you start giving yourself that space and your work risks becoming too bureaucratic. You have to encourage yourself constantly to be a creative and not to become just a manager. If you act otherwise, you'll be finished as an advertising creator.

Do you think advertising creators have a responsibility to the public?
Yes, absolutely! We enter people's world without being invited. We try to sell them things, ideas, ways of living. If you lack in social consciousness, you end up selling awful prejudices, you offend people unnecessarily, and you help to make society even worse. It is quite easy to make good, even daring advertising without forgetting that life is much larger than the ad.

In your opinion, do clients trust ad agencies as much as they should?
No. They mistrust agencies at

every turn. They are prepared to help us make mistakes and then say that those mistakes were only our fault. It is a hypocritical relationship that has only been getting worse down the decades.

What is the most unusual form you've seen an ad take (i.e. sidewalk ads, etc.)? Do you think it was effective?
I must confess I'm not much of an admirer of this kind of advertising. I've already seen some of that stuff, of course. But nothing that has thrilled me very much.

Which ad or campaign (by someone else) do you most admire?
The answer must seem obvious, but no one has made better advertising than Nike for the last 10 years.

Is there any subject or source material (politics, the Bible, the Beatles) that should be off-limits to advertisers?
As a rule, advertising can meddle with everything and everybody. The problem is the suitability of the idea and the way advertising interacts with sensitive matters. For example, I've already seen good ads using Nazism as a theme. On the other hand, I had to reprove a completely idiotic ad that tried to sell deodorant by using a photo of Nazis with their arms up. On this topic, as on everything else in life, it is common sense (so rarely found anywhere these days) that must command.

Is controversy a good thing for some advertisers?
It's the best thing in some cases. But, I guess, controversy is only positive if it was deliberate from the start or if it happens among people outside our target.

Do you think the West—particularly the US and UK—sets the pace for the rest of the world in advertising, or have other regions now taken the lead?
Yes and no. It was true some years ago. Nowadays, with our information society, references come from all over the world. From the quantitative point of view, the US will always take the lead. But, in terms of quality, sometimes I learn more from a single ad from Argentina or Brazil than I do from half a year of American and English work.

Will advertising continue to merge & blend with entertainment content—and is that a

good thing for the audience?
Oh yes! It's really good to see how advertising is becoming more and more capable of getting into entertainment content. It's a rather effective way of selling things to customers without annoying them too much.

Who was your past mentor/inspiration in advertising?
The never fading Bill Bernbach and David Ogilvy. Also the style of the former Fallon and much of the present Wieden + Kennedy.

Who do you most admire in your profession today?
I do admire the work of Marcelo Serpa at BBDO Brazil.

If an ad is well-liked by the public and wins awards, yet the product does not sell as a result, what (if anything) can we conclude from that?
That ad is the wrong one. There would probably be another kind of approach that the public would like better that could even win prizes while helping sell the product. The product might have problems too, but the agency should have been able to identify them and propose an advertising solution that would add value to it.

What will spark the next "Creative Revolution" in advertising?
Honestly, I'm not expecting a "Creative Revolution" in advertising. I expect some evolution. I hope advertisers will be able to face the challenge of communicating with a more and more well-informed, skeptical and dispersed society regarding psychographic characteristics. I would tell revolution fans to go to Cuba.

Over to you—any final thoughts on advertising?
When advertising is good, people even believe in eggs without shells.

At 36, Edson Athayde is currently the most honored individual in the history of Portuguese advertising, earning nearly 500 prizes in national and international festivals. In addition to his work in advertising, Athayde has been a newspaper columnist, the host of a prime-time advertising program on Portuguese television, a lecturer and a best-selling author. He is a shareholder, President and Creative Director at Edson FCB.

(opposite) Public Service Ads by Edson FCB

THEY SAY COMPUTERS WILL SUBSTITUTE BOOKS.

YEAH, SURE, HMM, HMM.

noticias
editorial

THE PLEASURE OF READING.

240 horsepower

Front-wheel drive

Satellite-Linked Navigation System

5-speed automatic transmission

VTEC engine

Best minivan on the road

240 laps around the block

Rear-wheel drive

Where's the fire?

1 speed (superfast)

Beans and franks

Not allowed in the street

When it comes to driving your kids around town, it's beyond compare. The Odyssey. **HONDA** A minivan. Only better.

DVD Entertainment System

Leather-trimmed seats

Wireless headphones

Third-row Magic Seat

Passengers ride in comfort

Bridle and blinders

Molded plastic saddle

Horse whinnies

Tail

Saddle sores

When it comes to keeping your kids happy, it's beyond compare. The Odyssey. **HONDA** A minivan. Only better.

Dual front airbags

Dual side airbags

Traction Control System

3-point seat belts for all 7 passengers

4-wheel anti-lock braking system

Quadruple 5-star safety rating

Padded steering wheel

10-inch-thick rubber bumper

Out of control

What seat belts?

Another car

Must be this tall to ride

When it comes to protecting your kids, it's beyond compare. The Odyssey. **HONDA** A minivan. Only better.

Space. It isn't as far away as you might have thought. The Civic. **HONDA**

"Uncle."

36 city. 44 highway. And that incredible feeling of beating the system. The Civic. **HONDA**

Introducing the 160-horsepower Civic Si. You'll know it when you see it. **HONDA**

Larry Postaer Art Director: Richard Bess, Photographer: Stephan Wilkes Copywriter: Pat Mendelson Art Buyer: Annie Ross Client: American Honda Motor Company   Automotive 16, 17

'Observatory,' 'Uncle' and 'Doors' Agency: Rubin Postaer and Associates Creative Director:

There will always be those who try to take the fun out of driving. Our proud rebuttal to these cynics is the 911 Carrera. Ignite the new 3.6 liter, 320 hp engine. Aim its re-sculpted front end at the horizon. And roam the curves of the earth. Contact us at 1-800-PORSCHE or porsche.com.

We don't know who invented speed bumps, but we're pretty sure he wasn't German.

Shimmering off flowing lines carved by the wind. Illuminating a spacious cockpit through a retractable glass roof. Yes, the new 911 Targa is a worthy destination for any ray of light. That said, a 320-hp boxer engine makes it an elusive one. Contact us at 1-800-PORSCHE or porsche.com.

The new 911 Targa. Occasionally, sunlight finds its 93-million mile journey worthwhile.

One ride in the 911 Turbo and you know. Not another car in the world could feel like this. Explosive, yet smooth to the redline. Fluid all-wheel drive imposes your will on the pavement. Certainty, is your choice of exquisite finishes. Contact us at 1-800-PORSCHE or porsche.com.

If you could own any car in the world, what color would you choose?

WHAT OBJECTS?

The hand-built, all-aluminum Acura NSX. As if a 290-horsepower VTEC™ engine, race-tuned suspension and Formula One heritage weren't enough, we enhanced its aerodynamic styling. The NSX. Nothing else comes close. ⒶACURA

Save the planet.

Fast.

There is a car, an electric car, that can accelerate quickly without a second of hesitation. It can maneuver easily through traffic. Speed up and over the steepest grade. And, most important, leave all your doubts far behind. That electric car is the EV1. The most aerodynamic production car ever built. Get in and don't look back. The world is depending on you. The EV1 from General Motors. Drive one at a Saturn retailer or contact us at 1.800.25ELECTRIC or gmev.com

EV1
ELECTRIC

Top speed: 183mph.

Not bad for a car with no engine.

An EV1 shattered the world electric-car land-speed record, reaching a speed most gas-powered cars can only dream of attaining. And while you'll experience the same instantaneous acceleration that propelled that historic prototype, the EV1 you can drive is electronically regulated to reach a more responsible speed. So you will still be able to recognize the world you are helping to save. The EV1 from General Motors. Drive one at a Saturn retailer or contact us at 1.800.25ELECTRIC or gmev.com

EV1
ELECTRIC

Listen to your doctor.
Listen to your wife.
Look after your heart.

The new 911 Cabriolet.

After 38 years of development,
we've come even one step closer to the 911.

The new 911.

Mona Lisa is just a painting.
Faust is just a book.
This is just a car.

The new 911 Cabriolet.

For more information, call the Porsche Information Centre on 0845 7 911 911 or visit www.porsche.com.

It's what roads are for.

The Boxster S.

PORSCHE

For more information, call the Porsche Information Centre on 0845 7 911 911 or visit www.porsche.com.

Who says honeymoons don't last?

The Boxster S.

PORSCHE

Automotive 22.23 Carlos Ferreira and Torsten Schöps Photographers: Peter Lavery and Georg Fischer Copywriters: David Steel and Sven Niemeyer Account Coordinators: David Steel and Sven Niemeyer Account Coordinators: Brigitte Kemper and: Marius Darschin Client: Dr. Ing. h.c. f. Porsche AG

YEREVAN	**7,013 MI.**
DHAKA	**8,668 MI.**
BALIKPAPAN	**10,047 MI.**
RUTA MAYA	**1,180 MI.**
SWAKOPMUND	**9,148 MI.**
QASR AL-MUSHATTA	**7,187 MI.**
OUAGADOUGOU	**6,161 MI.**
MBÉ	**7,743 MI.**
QAANAAQ	**3,334 MI.**
DJIBOUTI	**8,552 MI.**
MALL	**2 MI.**

Whichever way you go, you'll require a sturdy mode of transport. One capable of carrying all the treasures you may acquire. For some, a camel will do. But the well-seasoned traveler prefers something with a fresher scent. We recommend a new car smell, with just a hint of leather. Wend your way toward a Land Rover Centre, and see what a Range Rover is made.

LAND-ROVER

RANGE ROVER

230 hp V6 · Terrain sensing 4WD · THE AXIOM · ISUZU Go farther.

RESIDENT NON-CONFORMIST
21042 PINE ST
LOS ANGELES CA 90026-1001

'Non Conformist' Agency: Goodby, Silverstein & Partners Creative Directors: Jeffrey Goodby and Rich Silverstein Art Director: Christopher Gyorgy Photographer: Michael Rausch Copywriter: Mike McKay Client: American Isuzu Motors, Inc.

Harald Schmitt and Tom Tilliger Art Director: Florian Beck Photographer: Johannes G. Krzeslack Copywriter: Roland Wetzel Account Coordinators: Gerald Heinecke and Kirsten Specht Client: Deutsche Renault AG

'Eyes' Agency: Publicis Werbeagentur GmbH Creative Directors: Michael Boebel,

Der neue Polo lässt einen vieles leichter nehmen. Seine stabile Karosserie ist so ausgelegt, dass sich kleinere Schäden ohne großen Aufwand beseitigen lassen. Ein klarer Vorteil bei der Bewertung durch die Autoversicherer – sie stufen den Polo mit 47 kW (65 PS)-Benzinmotor in die Vollkaskoklasse 10 ein. Damit ist der neue Polo nicht nur konkurrenzlos günstig. Sondern lässt einen manches im Leben auch etwas unbesorgter sehen.

Durch nichts zu beeindrucken. **Der neue Polo.**

Gewinner Goldenes Lenkrad 2001

Mit dem neuen Polo fühlt man sich gegen alles gewappnet. Schon in der Grundausstattung verfügt er über Front- und Seiten-airbags, ABS und eine elektrohydraulische Servolenkung. Zusätzlich lässt er sich um Ausstattungsdetails erweitern, die in dieser Klasse nicht selbstverständlich sind – wie das Elektronische Stabilisierungsprogramm ESP, Lederausstattung oder Navigationssystem. Ein neues Selbstbewusstsein, das sich auch auf den Fahrer überträgt.

Durch nichts zu beeindrucken. **Der neue Polo.**

Gewinner Goldenes Lenkrad 2001

Der neue Polo fühlt sich jeder Aufgabe gewachsen. Fünf verschiedene Diesel- und Benzinmotoren passen sich individuell den unterschiedlichsten Anforderungen an. Von 47 kW (65 PS)-Benziner bis zum leistungsstarken 74 kW (100 PS)-TDI¹ zeichnen sie sich alle durch optimale Wirtschaftlichkeit aus. Und erfüllen schon heute die strengen Abgasnormen von morgen. Ein Gefühl von Überlegenheit, das sich direkt auf den Fahrer überträgt.

Durch nichts zu beeindrucken. **Der neue Polo.**

Gewinner Goldenes Lenkrad 2001

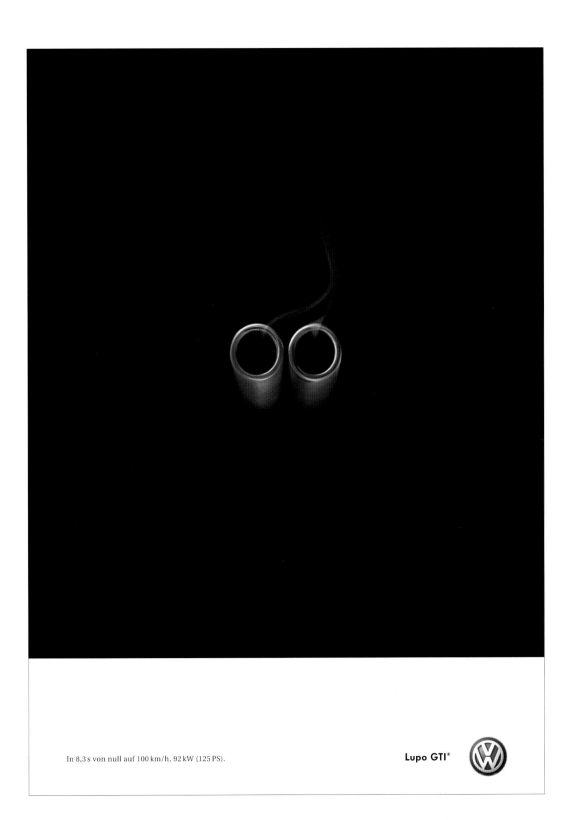

In 8,3 s von null auf 100 km/h, 92 kW (125 PS).

Lupo GTI®

Peace of mind.

Engineered for the Autobahn.

Smile if you own a set.

They're not just tires.
They're Continental tires.™

In harmony with the road.

Ontinental⊛
They're not just tires.
They're Continental tires.™

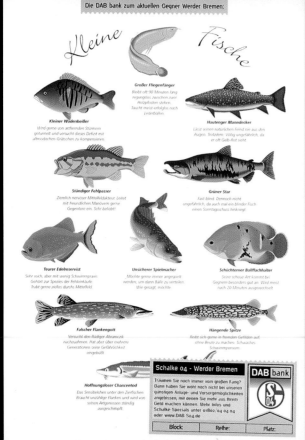

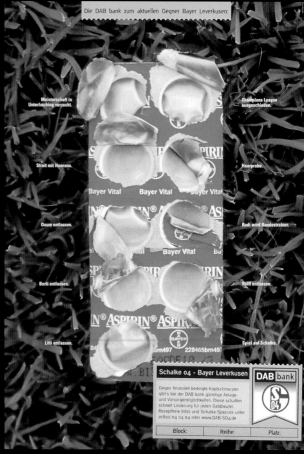

Bank of America
The official bank of the U.S. Olympic team

Bank of America
The official bank of the U.S. Olympic team

'Ski Jumper' and 'Hockey' Agency: Bozell New York Creative Director: Tony Granger Art Director: Lori Sibal Photographer: Leen Thijsse Copywriter: Ed Johnson Group Creative Directors: Glenn Batkin and Brett Howlett Client: Bank of America

Every revolution has its color.

Wella. Beautiful hair needs an expert.

'Revolution' Agency: Jung von Matt/Alster GmbH Creative Directors: Deneke von Weltzen and Alexander Gutt

6 seconds of flaming light.

6 weeks of flaming color and longer.

Wella. Beautiful hair needs an expert.

'Match' Agency: Jung von Matt/Alster GmbH Creative Directors: Deneke von Weltzien and Alexander Gutt Art Directors: Gertrude Eisele and Sabine Jantzen Designers: Christine Ratsch and Christiane Huwer Photographers: Michael Wirth and Tom Kleineberg

Beautiful hair needs an expert. In Japan and 147 other countries.

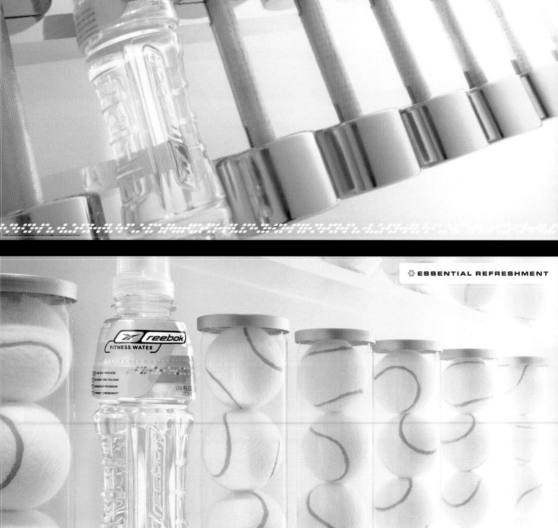

Agency: Karacters Design Group Creative Director: Maria Kennedy Art Director: Matthew Clark Designer: Matthew Clark Photographer: Raeff Miles Copywriter: Randy Stein Account Coordinator: Brynn Wanstall Client: Clearly Canadian Beverage Corp.

Proud Sponsor of the US Open.

Enjoy Heineken Responsibly www.heineken.com ©2001 HEINEKEN® Lager Beer. Heineken USA Inc., White Plains, NY

Beverages **42,43**

'Tennis Can' Agency: Lowe Creative Directors: Gary Goldsmith and Dean Hacohen Art Director: Niko Courtelis Photographer: Dennis Blachut Copywriter: David Lowe Client: Heineken USA

got chocolate milk?

Joy to the world. Chocolate milk is good for you.

got chocolate milk

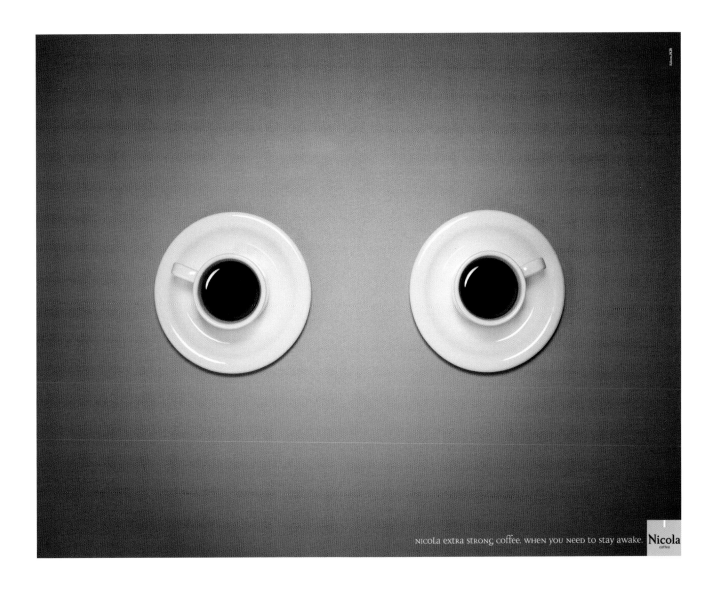

Rediscover flight.

MUSEUM OF FLIGHT
5 minutes south of downtown | museumofflight.org

RED IS THE COLOR OF REVOLUTION

REGENCY

VERTICAL VENTURES
CLIMBING GYM
813.884.ROCK

390178

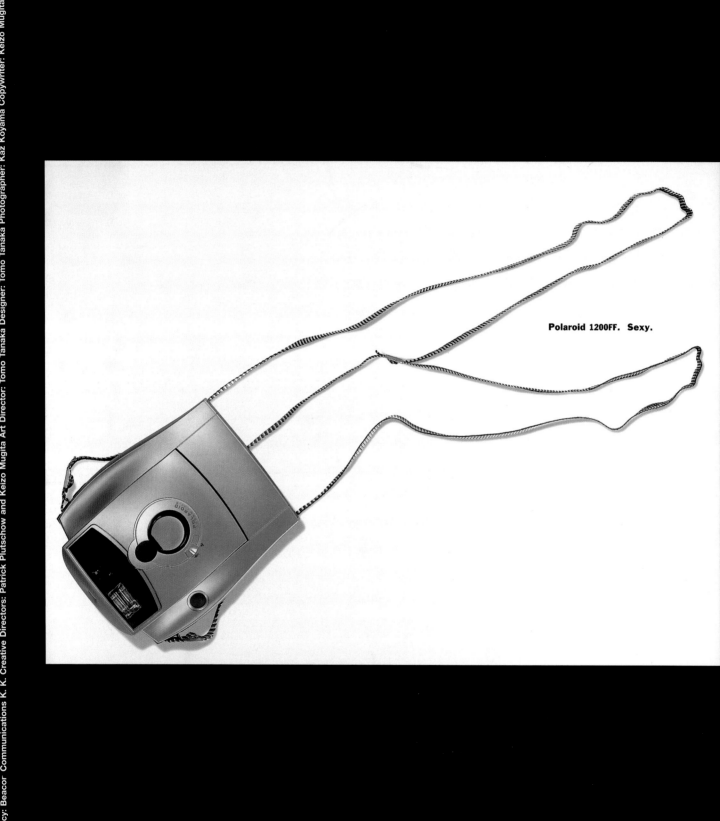

Polaroid 1200FF. Sexy.

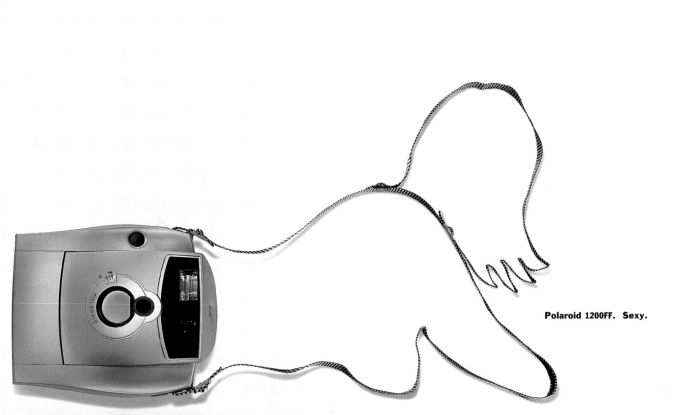

Polaroid 1200FF. Sexy.

THE SPIRIT MOUNTAIN CASINO EXPANSION PROJECT.
IT'S BIGGER. IT'S BETTER. IT'S OPENING SOON.

SPIRIT
MOUNTAIN
CASINO

Hwy. 18, Grand Ronde. 1-800-760-7977. www.spiritmountain.com

THE SPIRIT MOUNTAIN CASINO EXPANSION PROJECT.
IT'S BIGGER. IT'S BETTER. IT'S OPENING SOON.

SPIRIT
MOUNTAIN
CASINO

Hwy. 18, Grand Ronde. 1-800-760-7977. www.spiritmountain.com

LUCK HAPPENS

You never know when luck will strike at Oregon's most popular casino. Located about an hour from Portland and less than 30 minutes from the coast, you'll find casino games galore, 5 restaurants and a 100-room lodge. For more information, call 1-800-760-7977.

SPIRIT
MOUNTAIN
CASINO

HWY 18 • GRAND RONDE • WWW.SPIRITMOUNTAIN.COM

LUCK HAPPENS

Anything's possible at Oregon's top attraction and most popular casino. Open 24 hours a day, you'll find tons of casino space, 5 restaurants, live entertainment and a 100-room lodge. All located about an hour from Portland. For more information, call 1-800-760-7977.

SPIRIT
MOUNTAIN
CASINO

HWY 18 • GRAND RONDE, OR • WWW.SPIRITMOUNTAIN.COM

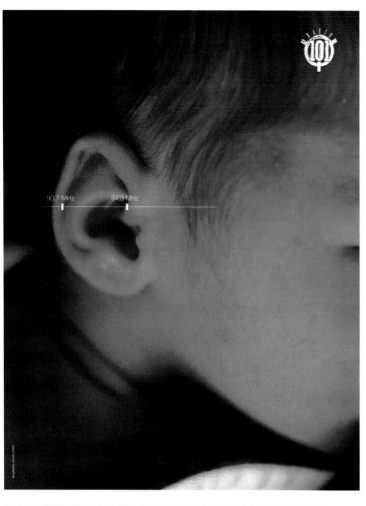

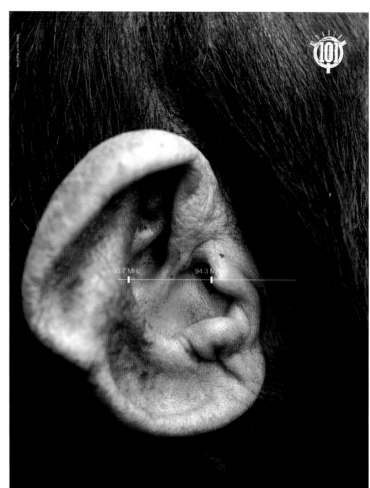

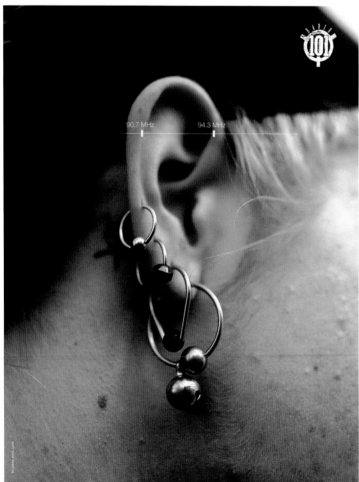

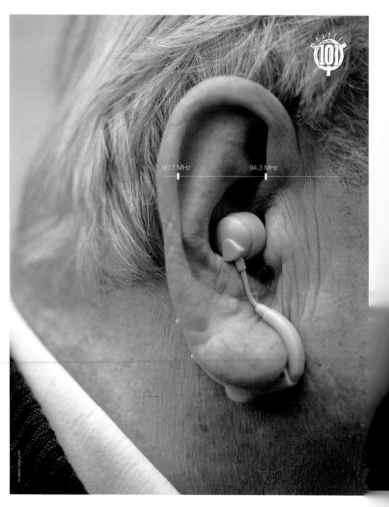

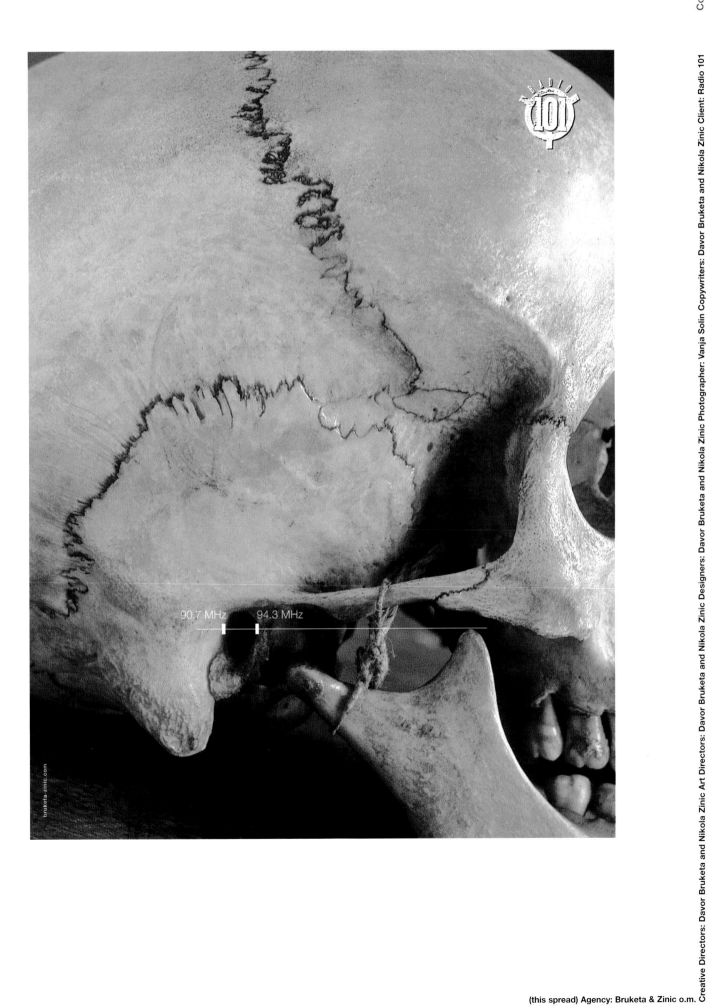

90.7 MHz   94.3 MHz

bruketa-zinic.com

Creative Directors: Davor Bruketa and Nikola Zinic Art Directors: Davor Bruketa and Nikola Zinic Designers: Davor Bruketa and Nikola Zinic Photographer: Vanja Solin Copywriters: Davor Bruketa and Nikola Zinic Client: Radio 101

(this spread) Agency: Bruketa & Zinic o.m.

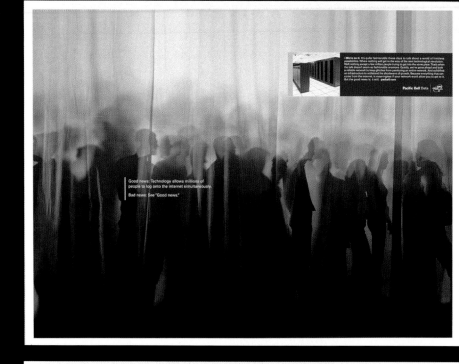

Good luck in the playoffs, Spurs. We could really use another one.

Southwestern Bell |

Proud Sponsor of the San Antonio Spurs

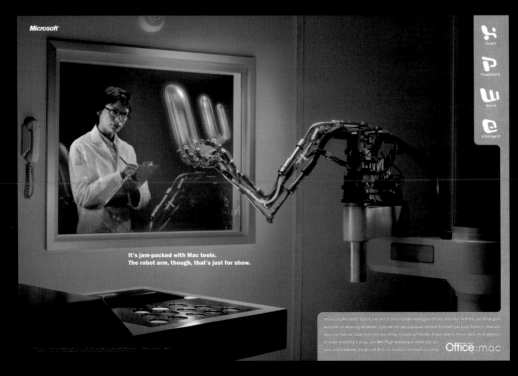

ACCURATE COLOR. THE LACIE ELECTRONBLUE III MONITOR. LaCie

color matching system

PROCESS COATED

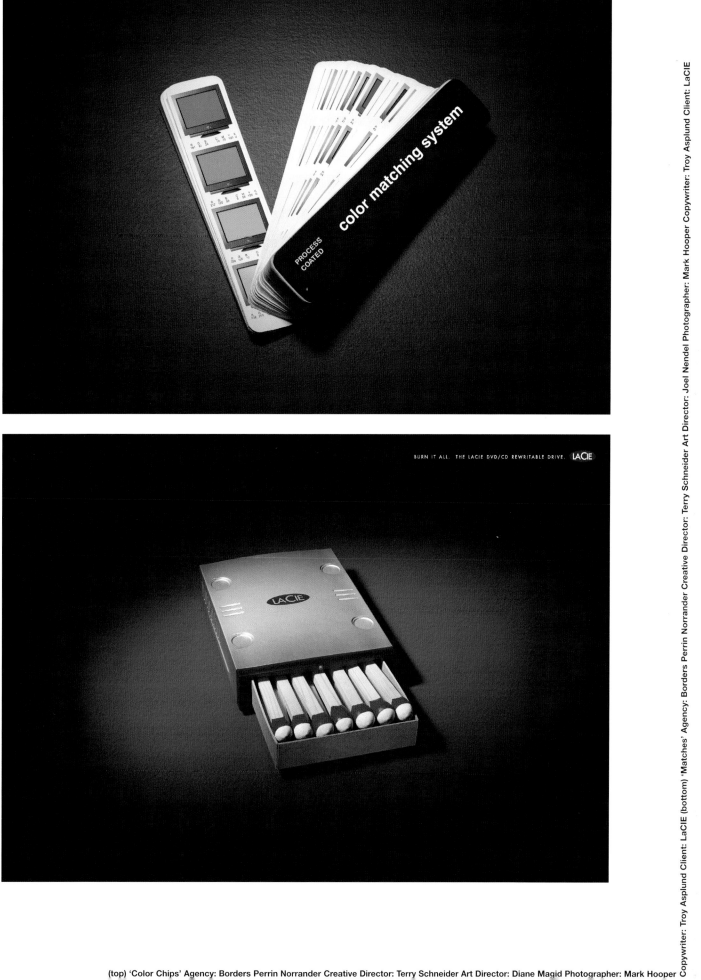

BURN IT ALL. THE LACIE DVD/CD REWRITABLE DRIVE. LaCie

LaCie

Copywriter: Troy Asplund Client: LaCie (bottom) 'Matches' Agency: Borders Perrin Norrander Creative Director: Terry Schneider Art Director: Joel Nendel Photographer: Mark Hooper Copywriter: Troy Asplund Client: LaCie   Computer Software **56, 57**

(top) 'Color Chips' Agency: Borders Perrin Norrander Creative Director: Terry Schneider Art Director: Diane Magid Photographer: Mark Hooper Copywriter:

BECAUSE THIS ALARM

DOESN'T HAVE A SNOOZE BUTTON.

It's easy to get up in the morning and stay up late when you're a GE-powered

aircraft, because the affordable F110 engine stays on wing longer.

GE Aircraft Engines

www.geae.com

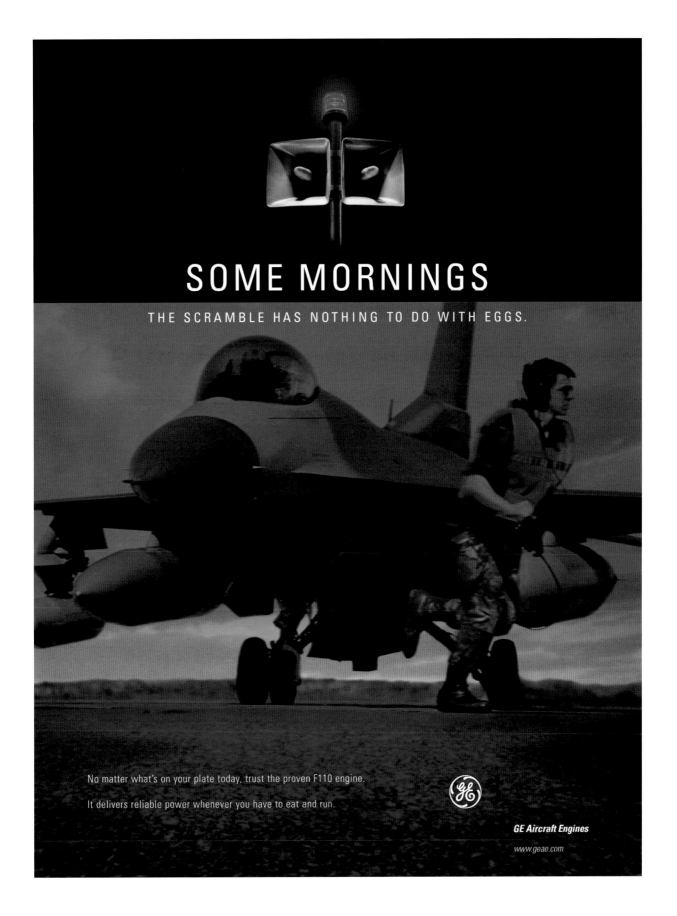

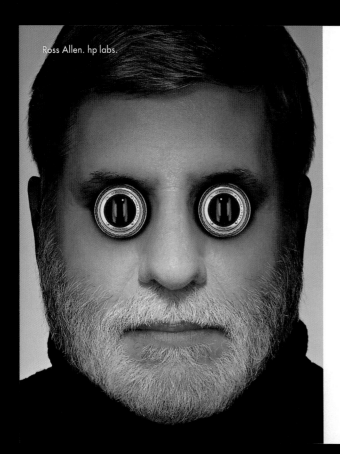

Ross Allen. hp labs.

Your eyes never take a bad picture.

This simple fact is the inspiration behind the next generation
digital cameras Ross is inventing. Powered by image processing chips designed to
work like the human eye, they automatically balance colors and
compensate for poor lighting conditions. So when it comes to your pictures at least,
what you see is what you get.
www.hp.com

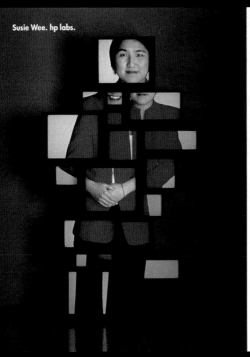

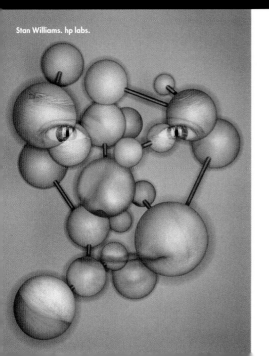

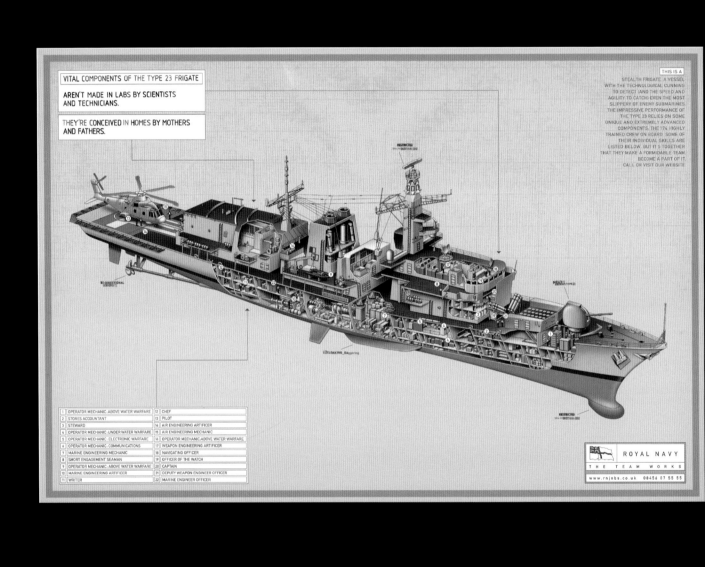

VITAL COMPONENTS OF THE TYPE 23 FRIGATE

AREN'T MADE IN LABS BY SCIENTISTS AND TECHNICIANS.

THEY'RE CONCEIVED IN HOMES BY MOTHERS AND FATHERS.

THIS IS A
STEALTH FRIGATE. A VESSEL WITH THE TECHNOLOGICAL CUNNING TO DETECT (AND THE SPEED AND AGILITY TO CATCH) EVEN THE MOST SLIPPERY OF ENEMY SUBMARINES. THE IMPRESSIVE PERFORMANCE OF THE TYPE 23 RELIES ON SOME UNIQUE AND EXTREMELY ADVANCED COMPONENTS. THE 174 HIGHLY TRAINED CREW ON BOARD. SOME OF THEIR INDIVIDUAL SKILLS ARE LISTED BELOW. BUT IT'S TOGETHER THAT THEY MAKE A FORMIDABLE TEAM. BECOME A PART OF IT. CALL OR VISIT OUR WEBSITE.

1	OPERATOR MECHANIC: ABOVE WATER WARFARE	12	CHEF
2	STORES ACCOUNTANT	13	PILOT
3	STEWARD	14	AIR ENGINEERING ARTIFICER
4	OPERATOR MECHANIC: UNDER WATER WARFARE	15	AIR ENGINEERING MECHANIC
5	OPERATOR MECHANIC: ELECTRONIC WARFARE	16	OPERATOR MECHANIC: ABOVE WATER WARFARE
6	OPERATOR MECHANIC: COMMUNICATIONS	17	WEAPON ENGINEERING ARTIFICER
7	MARINE ENGINEERING MECHANIC	18	NAVIGATING OFFICER
8	SHORT ENGAGEMENT SEAMAN	19	OFFICER OF THE WATCH
9	OPERATOR MECHANIC: ABOVE WATER WARFARE	20	CAPTAIN
10	MARINE ENGINEERING ARTIFICER	21	DEPUTY WEAPON ENGINEER OFFICER
11	WRITER	22	MARINE ENGINEER OFFICER

ROYAL NAVY
THE TEAM WORKS
www.rnjobs.co.uk 08456 07 55 55

MARINE ENGINEER | ARTIFICER | NURSE | OPERATOR MECHANIC | PILOT | WARFARE OFFICER | STEWARD

AWESOMELY POWERFUL.
DEADLY ACCURATE.

BUT WITHOUT HIGHLY TRAINED
WEAPONS SPECIALISTS
ABOUT AS LETHAL AS A
PORK SAUSAGE.

CLASSIFIED
000000090/1

WARHEAD
450 PAYLOAD

THE HARPOON

ONE OF THE FOXIEST, COSTLIEST
GUIDED MISSILES IN THE WORLD.
FROM A RANGE OF 70 MILES,
IT CAN STOP A 4800 TONNE ENEMY
VESSEL DEAD IN THE WATER.

BUT THE MOST VITAL PART OF
THE HARPOON ISN'T ITS HIGHLY
SOPHISTICATED INERTIAL GUIDANCE
SYSTEM. IT'S THE HIGHLY TRAINED
INDIVIDUALS WHO UNDERSTAND
HOW THE THING WORKS. AND KEEP
IT IN BATTLE READY CONDITION.

THEY'RE PART OF A VITAL TEAM.
JOIN THEM. CALL OR VISIT OUR WEBSITE.

RESTRICTED

ROYAL NAVY
THE TEAM WORKS
www.rnjobs.co.uk 08456 07 55 55

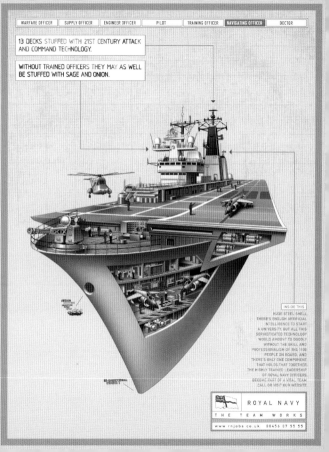

WARFARE OFFICER | SUPPLY OFFICER | ENGINEER OFFICER | PILOT | TRAINING OFFICER | NAVIGATING OFFICER | DOCTOR

13 DECKS STUFFED WITH 21ST CENTURY ATTACK
AND COMMAND TECHNOLOGY.

WITHOUT TRAINED OFFICERS THEY MAY AS WELL
BE STUFFED WITH SAGE AND ONION.

INSIDE THIS

HUGE STEEL SHELL,
THERE'S ENOUGH ARTIFICIAL
INTELLIGENCE TO START
A UNIVERSITY. BUT ALL THIS
SOPHISTICATED TECHNOLOGY
WOULD AMOUNT TO DIDDLY
WITHOUT THE SKILL AND
PROFESSIONALISM OF THE 1100
PEOPLE ON BOARD. AND
THERE'S ONLY ONE COMPONENT
THAT HOLDS THAT TOGETHER.
THE HIGHLY TRAINED LEADERSHIP
OF ROYAL NAVY OFFICERS.
BECOME PART OF A VITAL TEAM.
CALL OR VISIT OUR WEBSITE.

BI-DIRECTIONAL

ROYAL NAVY
THE TEAM WORKS
www.rnjobs.co.uk 08456 07 55 55

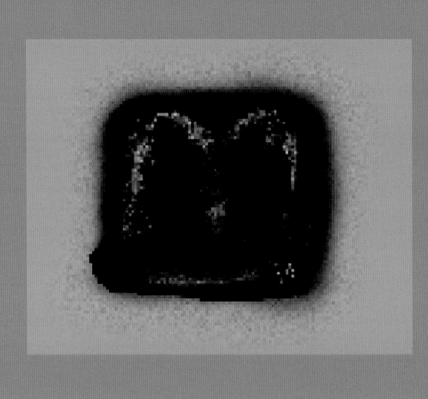

锦上自己の品味。

锦上來自日本の人氣限量版

IBM
ThinkPad s31

IBM.

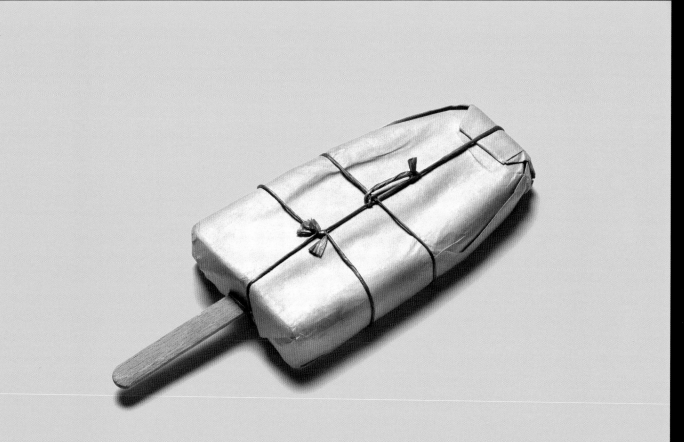

Deutsche Post
EXPRESS

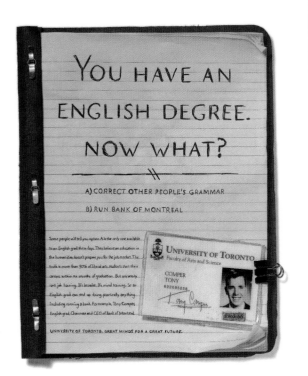

The School of Visual Concepts.

206·623·1560

'Bean Brain' Agency: DDB Seattle Creative Director: Fred Hammerquist Art Director: Larry Olson Designer: Todd Hofmeister Client: School of Visual Concepts   Education 66,67

[hp photosmart 618 digital camera]

Film. Man, the 1900s were fun.

Presenting digital photography's leap from infancy to adulthood. A camera
that shows you your pictures instantly. Pictures artfully captured with the help
of our engineers' remarkable chip. And an invention that mimics the most
sophisticated lens of all: the human eye. For more information on our entire
collection of digital imaging products, visit www.hp.com/go/photography

[hp jornada 565]

Introducing a choice in hip new office spaces. Lefty or righty.

Presenting the essentials of an office in the palm of your hand. A state-of-the-art PDA
that thinks like a laptop, with Internet, organizational software, and Microsoft®
applications. At last, your mobile office will truly be complete. For more information on
our entire collection of home office products, visit www.hp.com/go/information

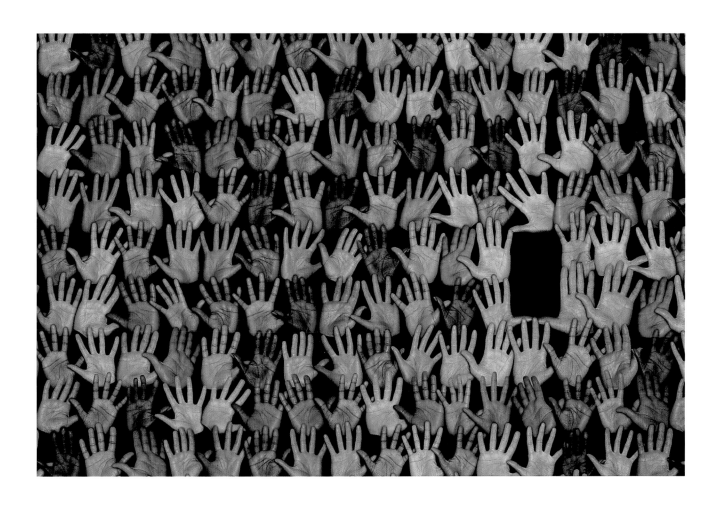

WIDESCREEN TV BY **Panasonic**

T[tau]PB WITH SURROUND SOUND BY **Panasonic**

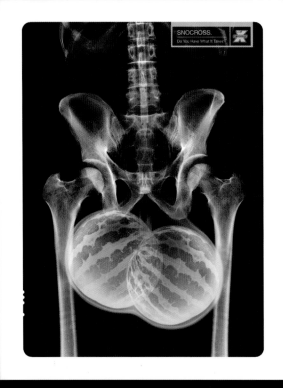

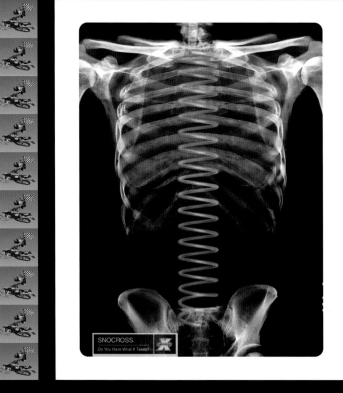

Call for entries. By January 11, 2002

Call for entries. By January 11, 2002

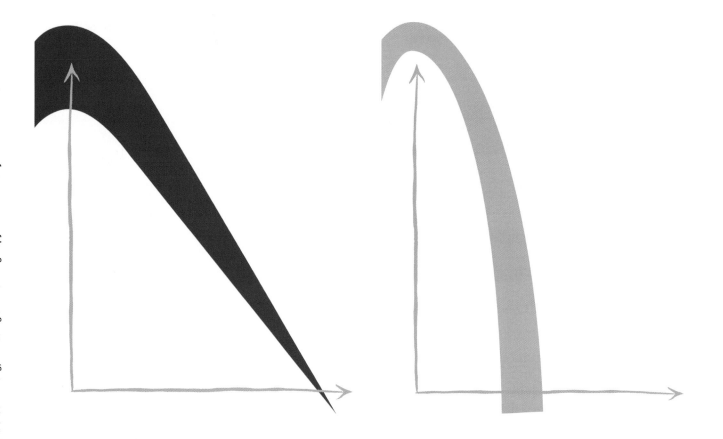

Agency: Bartle Bogle Hegarty Creative Director: Steve Elrick Art Director: Alex Lim Designers: David Wong, Brenda Ng and Wan Ying Copywriter: Tinus Strydom Account Coordinator: Chris Harris Client: Institute of Advertising Singapore

BIG BRANDS BIG TROUBLE?
JACK TROUT ADDRESSES THE SINGAPORE INTERNATIONAL ADVERTISING CONGRESS

BIG BRANDS BIG TROUBLE?
JACK TROUT ADDRESSES THE SINGAPORE INTERNATIONAL ADVERTISING CONGRESS

Proud sponsor of the Toronto International Film Festival. **Drivers wanted.** VW

Proud sponsor of the Toronto International Film Festival. **Drivers wanted.** VW

Proud sponsor of the Toronto International Film Festival. **Drivers wanted.** VW

Proud sponsor of the Toronto International Film Festival. **Drivers wanted.** VW

Agency: Arnold Worldwide Art Director: Kevin Dailor Photographer: Craig Cutler Client: Volkswagen

⊛ NEW YORK, N.Y. He was flying a mail route from Chicago to St. Louis when he first heard about it. A $25,000 prize to anyone who could fly nonstop from New York City to Paris. Charles Lindbergh, a barnstormer from the woods of Minnesota, was determined to claim it. • After rounding up money for a plane, he chose a specially modified Ryan Monoplane. To keep weight down and make room for fuel, instrumentation and creature comforts were kept to a bare minimum. When completed, the Spartan craft of wood, cloth and metal could hold 400 gallons of the precious juice that would carry him across the ocean. In honor of his backers, Lindbergh dubbed the Ryan N-X 211 "The Spirit of St. Louis."

After his takeoff, the world followed his progress as best they could. Headlines appeared in Berlin, Tokyo, London, Paris and all across America. All humanity was rooting for him to succeed. For his success was mankind's success. An impossible gauntlet had been thrown down, and human courage would pick it up. • He was last seen over St. John's, Newfoundland. And then... nothing, as he headed into the great

WAS IT FAIR TO CALL IT A SOLO FLIGHT WHEN HE CARRIED THE DREAMS OF MILLIONS WITH HIM?

He was now ready. • After arriving in New York during foul weather, he waited days for the skies to clear. But it continued to rain, turning the airstrip at Roosevelt Field on Long Island into a soggy, muddy morass. • Finally, there was a clearing. Despite a sleepless night, he decided to make a run at it. On the morning of May 20, 1927, with several hundred onlookers and journalists watching, he soared off to a fate unknown. Alone. With nothing beside him but a few sandwiches, some water, and his maps. •

CHARLES LINDBERGH AND HIS SPIRIT OF ST. LOUIS. FIRST NON-STOP TRANSATLANTIC FLIGHT. NEW YORK TO PARIS IN 36 HOURS.

watery void known as the Atlantic Ocean. At that point, he was alone in the world, out of contact with the rest of the planet for the next 15 hours. Then, off the left side of the plane, Ireland! Exhilarated by the sight of land, he knew he would make it. • At 10:24PM on May 21 – 33 hours, 30 minutes, and 3,610 miles after his departure – he landed at Le Bourget Field, where he was greeted by 150,000 cheering Parisians. • He'd battled exhaustion, hallucinations, bad weather, and the odds. But he'd done it. He'd flown from New York to Paris, alone. He had left the ground a relative unknown, and had landed the most famous man in the world. ⊛ PARIS, FRANCE

CELEBRATING 100 YEARS OF FLIGHT · FIRST FLIGHT CENTENNIAL COMMISSION · VISIT WWW.FIRSTFLIGHT.ORG

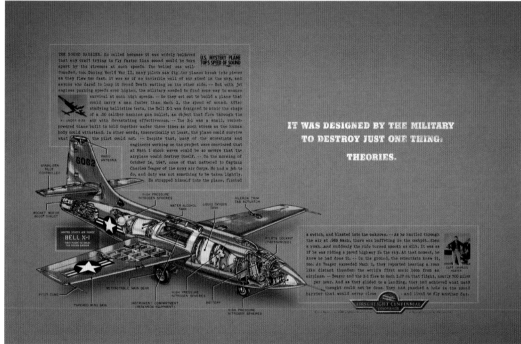

IT WAS DESIGNED BY THE MILITARY TO DESTROY JUST ONE THING:

THEORIES.

JULY 20, 1969

SEVEN CONTINENTS BECOME ONE PLANET.

We offer a number
of traditional styles.
(That number is,
of course, zero.)
Western shirts for untraditional men and
women everywhere. Call 1-800-514-1994.
BARN FLY

Some of the
best cowboys aren't
boys at all.

Knock-out Western skirts and shirts for untraditional women everywhere. Call 1-800-514-1994.
BARN FLY
Ranch Collection

The downside is,
it may compete with
your belt buckle.
Western shirts for untraditional men and
women everywhere. Call 1-800-514-1994.
BARN FLY

We beat up the
polo guy and
took his saddle.
Western shirts for untraditional men and
women everywhere. Call 1-800-514-1994.
BARN FLY

THE ORIGINAL *DJ QUIETSTORM*

THE ORIGINAL **ENGINEERED JEANS**

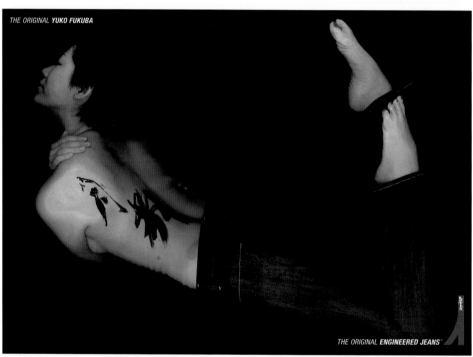

THE ORIGINAL *YUKO FUKUBA*

THE ORIGINAL **ENGINEERED JEANS**

THE ORIGINAL *PATRICK OANCIA*

THE ORIGINAL **ENGINEERED JEANS**

THE ORIGINAL *AKIRA OSAWA*

THE ORIGINAL *ENGINEERED JEANS*™

available at select macy's . keds.com

new tricks in **keds stretch**

keds

every wear

available at select macy's . keds.com

on a roll in **keds stretch**

keds

every wear

keds

every wear™

light gardening in **keds stretch**™

freewheeling in **keds stretch**™

keds

every wear™

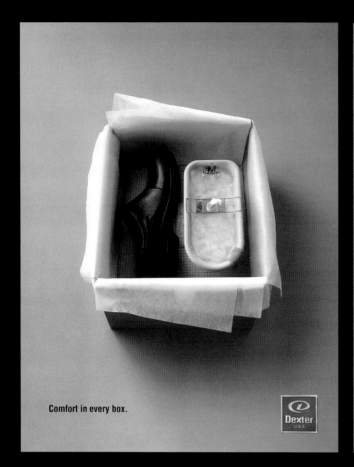

Comfort in every box.

Comfort in every box.

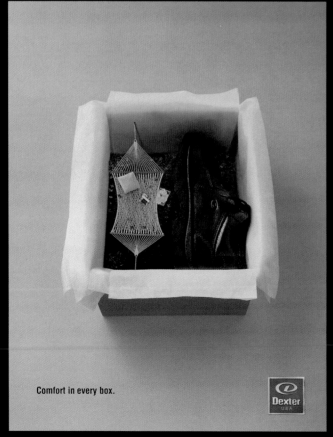

Comfort in every box.

Comfort in every box.

'Tub,' 'Popcorn,' 'Hammock' and 'Couch' Agency: Mullen Creative Directors: Michael Ancevic, Edward Boches and Stephen Mietelski Art Directors: Michael Ancevic Designer: Michael Ancevic Photographer: Michael Ancevic Photographer: Phillip Habib Copywriters: Mark

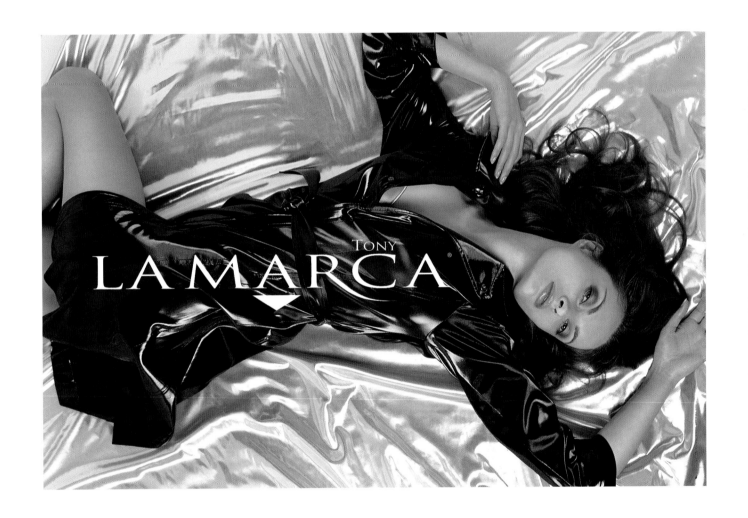

'Winter 2001 Collection' Agency: Signland Creative Director: Philippe Martins Art Director: Yvan Balsamo Designer: Yvan Balsamo Photographer: Christopher Ichou Client: Tony La March   Fashion 86,87

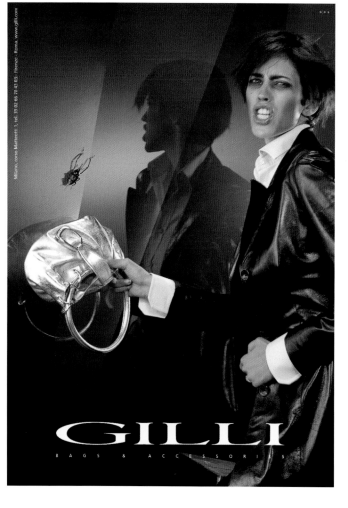

YOU KNOW THAT FAVORITE

SUMMER SPOT?

IT'S JUST A SWEATER AWAY

FROM BEING YOUR FAVORITE

FALL SPOT.

Stay outside for every moment of nature's performance this fall. All you need to do is dress warm, find that comfortable place you like to call your own, then relax and take in all the unfolding beauty of the season. Of course, you might want to consider a little help from L.L.Bean. Our jackets, fleecewear and other fall apparel have an ability for turning chilly days into pleasant ones. Our catalog is also filled with products to help prepare your family and home for fall. Call for a free copy or visit our website. You'll find the changing season doesn't have to change what you love about being outdoors.

Get your FREE FALL CATALOG. Call 1-800-221-4221 or visit us at www.llbean.com

L.L.Bean
start here
GO ANYWHERE

IT'S THAT TIME OF YEAR WHEN

GRASS TURNS GREEN,

GEESE FLY NORTH

AND YOU INSTINCTIVELY MIGRATE BACK TO

THE END OF THE DOCK.

We all have that certain place outdoors that feels like where we belong. Now that a new season is upon us, it's time to migrate to your spot and ponder the warm-weather pleasures ahead. Whatever your plans, L.L.Bean has the gear to make them even better. Furniture that invites you to relax. Clothing that intuitively knows the outdoors. Equipment that's as ready for an adventure as you are. Call for a free spring catalog or come explore our website to find what you need for the season. Then follow your best instincts outside. Nature has a place waiting for you. And you don't need to make any reservations.

For a FREE SPRING CATALOG call 1-800-558-4288 or visit us at www.llbean.com

L.L.Bean
start here
GO ANYWHERE

THE SUN IS BACK.

YOU REMEMBER HIM.

HE SPENT THE

PAST 6 MONTHS

WINTERING WITH YOUR PARENTS

IN FLORIDA.

The sun is starting its climb to the top of the sky again. It makes you want to step outside, throw up your arms and shout, "Welcome home!" Even better, you could go on a nice long hike together. At L.L.Bean, we've got whatever you want to take along on the journey. Gear that has a genuine understanding of what it takes to function in the natural world. Clothing and shoes that are comfortable enough to live in all summer long. Call for our free catalog or visit our website to start making your plans. Summer stretches out lazily in front of you. The days are long. Make the most of them.

For a FREE SPRING CATALOG call 1-800-558-4288 or visit us at www.llbean.com

L.L.Bean
start here
GO ANYWHERE

NO VINYL CREATURES WERE HARMED IN THE MAKING OF THIS GARMENT.

The undiluted freedom of pure premium leather. Every detail built for pure riding comfort. Harley-Davidson® MotorClothes™ riding leathers. Only at your nearest dealer. 1-800-LUV2RIDE. Or www.harley-davidson.com.

WATERPROOF. AIR VENTS. BETTER CLIMATE CONTROL THAN YOUR LAST MOTEL ROOM.

Built to repel what the road kicks up. It is your body armor. Yet perfectly detailed for all-day comfort. Harley-Davidson® MotorClothes™ riding leathers. Only at your dealer. 1-800-LUV2RIDE. Or www.harley-davidson.com.

EVERY CREASE TELLS A STORY. THE BASIC PLOT GOES LIKE THIS: HERO RIDES FAR AWAY.

Built to blow out of town. Sturdy leather. Front and back vents. Snap-down collar. Harley-Davidson® MotorClothes™ riding leathers. Only at your nearest dealer. 1-800-LUV2RIDE. Or www.harley-davidson.com.

Collar variations, machine: CMT 211 [semi-jacquard options] → Knits collars, trimmings, button-hole loops, yard goods and fabric pieces with simple patterning.

Pattern versatility / diagonal stitch groups, machine: CMS 330 TC 4 [with additional beds] → Knits double-faced fabrics: with Petinet effects, cable stitches and diagonal stitch groups. Maximum productivity even in the areas of narrowings.

Creative Director: Boris Pollig Art Director: Petra Ullrich Photographer: Juergen Altmann Copywriter: Jeanette Ottmar Account Supervisor: Jörg Dambacher Account Coordinator: Silke Schmidt Client: Stoll GmbH and Co.

Agency: RTS Rieger Team

Written by Willy Russell, Directed by Bruce Paltrow, Starring Edward Herrmann and Jacqueline McKenzie

Williamstown Theatre Festival
MICHAEL RITCHIE, PRODUCER

Educating Rita

June 27 – July 8

WTF Box Office: 413-597-3400 | www.WTFestival.org

W '01 Season

POWER CAN BE HELD
IN THE SMALLEST OF THINGS

THE TRILOGY BEGINS DECEMBER 2001

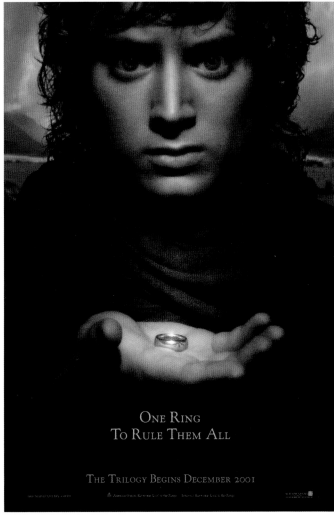

ONE RING
TO RULE THEM ALL

THE TRILOGY BEGINS DECEMBER 2001

Agency: The Ant Farm Creative Director: Julian Hills Art Director: Julian Hills Copywriter: J.R.R. Tolkien Digital Finisher: Daniel Clark Client: New Line Cinema

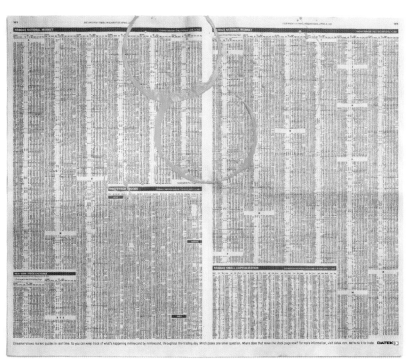

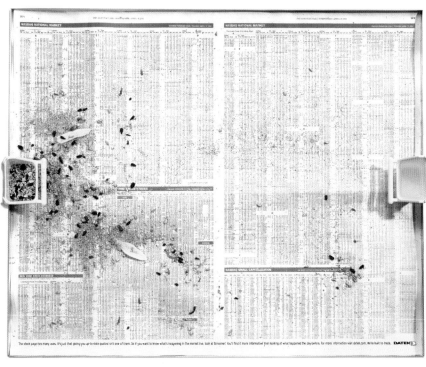

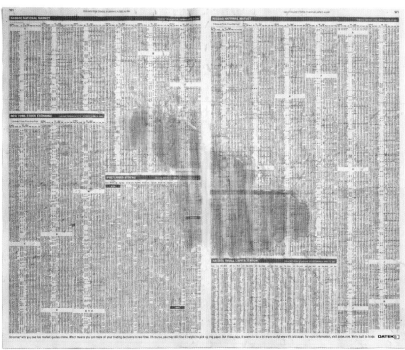

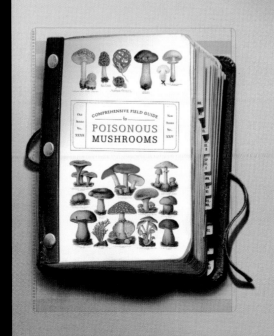

GONE WORKIN'

A GREAT 401(k) PLAN CAN REALLY HELP MOTIVATE PEOPLE. They work harder. They stay at their jobs longer. We should know. As the nation's 401(k) leader, we've been helping growing businesses and their employees secure their financial futures for over 50 years. No wonder more companies choose The Principal® for their 401(k) plans.* Investment choice and education, record keeping, loan services and asset allocation—we've got what you need. With personalized service and local support to make the process easy. Fishing for a better 401(k) plan? One of our representatives will be happy to catch your call at 1-800-986-3343 (ext. 80080).

WE UNDERSTAND WHAT YOU'RE WORKING FOR℠

www.principal.com

'Boat' Agency: Publicis in MidAmerica Creative Directors: Clifford Goodenough and Jim Newcombe Photographer: John McCallum Copywriter: Jim Newcombe Client: Principle Financial

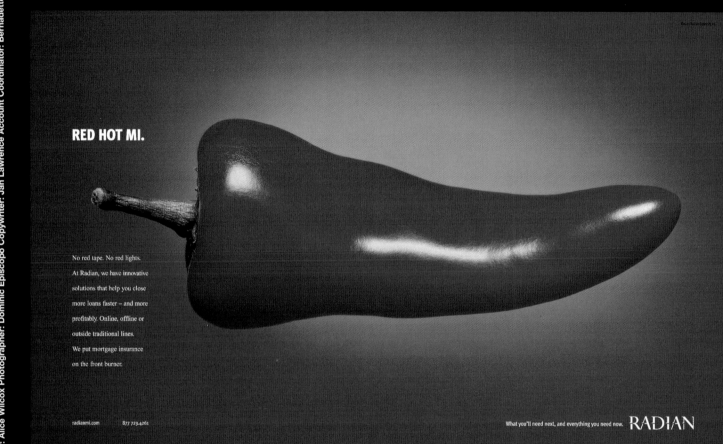

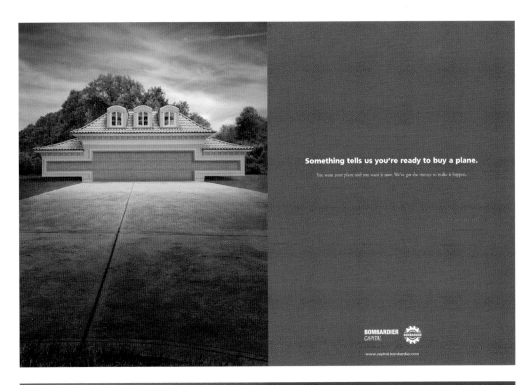

Something tells us you're ready to buy a plane.

You want your plane and you want it now. We've got the money to make it happen.

BOMBARDIER
CAPITAL

www.capital.bombardier.com

Something tells us you're ready to buy a plane.

We've got the money you need to get your deal—and your plane—off the ground.

BOMBARDIER
CAPITAL

www.capital.bombardier.com

Something tells us you're ready to buy a plane.

Get the money you need to get the plane you want. You're ready. And so are we.

BOMBARDIER
CAPITAL

www.capital.bombardier.com

Agency: Kelliher Samets Volk Creative Director: Bill Drew Art Director: Seth Drury Designer: Seth Drury Photographer: Sean W. Hennessy Copywriter: Bill Drew Location Scout: Andy Cox Client: Bombardier Capital Company

Financial 98,99

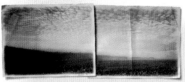

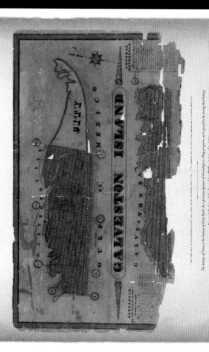

COLONEL FROST ALWAYS HAD

ONE EYE ON THE FUTURE AND

ONE EYE ON THE PAST

★

[Good thing he didn't drive a car]

*T*exas was in its infancy when our founder, Colonel T. C. Frost, made his very first loan. 133 years later, the lessons he learned while helping to build this fledgling state are still guiding us forward. And forward is indeed the operative word. The way we see it, the future is as wide open today as it was back in 1868. Opportunity abounds. But when you're the largest independent financial institution in Texas, opportunity does bring a certain responsibility. To hold steadfast to your principles. To never stop building on what came before. To provide real banking choices for Texans and their businesses. At Frost Bank, the choices have truly never been more diverse. Many of our customers now save time — and trees — with our sophisticated online banking services. Others look to us for customized estate and financial planning. And since everybody needs a little peace of mind, we even offer a full range of private and commercial insurance products. That's right, insurance through a bank. Right now you're probably wondering how a company steeped in such old-fashioned ideals could at the same time be a trailblazer. Well, isn't it obvious? We grew up in Texas.

Frost Bank
WE'RE FROM HERE

TO LEARN MORE ABOUT US, PLEASE VISIT WWW.FROSTBANK.COM.

"THE 1837 MAP OF TEXAS WITH PARTS OF THE ADJOINING STATES" WAS ADOPTED BY GERALD L. ATKINSON.

The history of Texas is the history of Frost Bank. As a primary sponsor of the Adopt-a-Map program, we're proud to be saving that history. You can help. Just call the General Land Office at 512-463-5169.

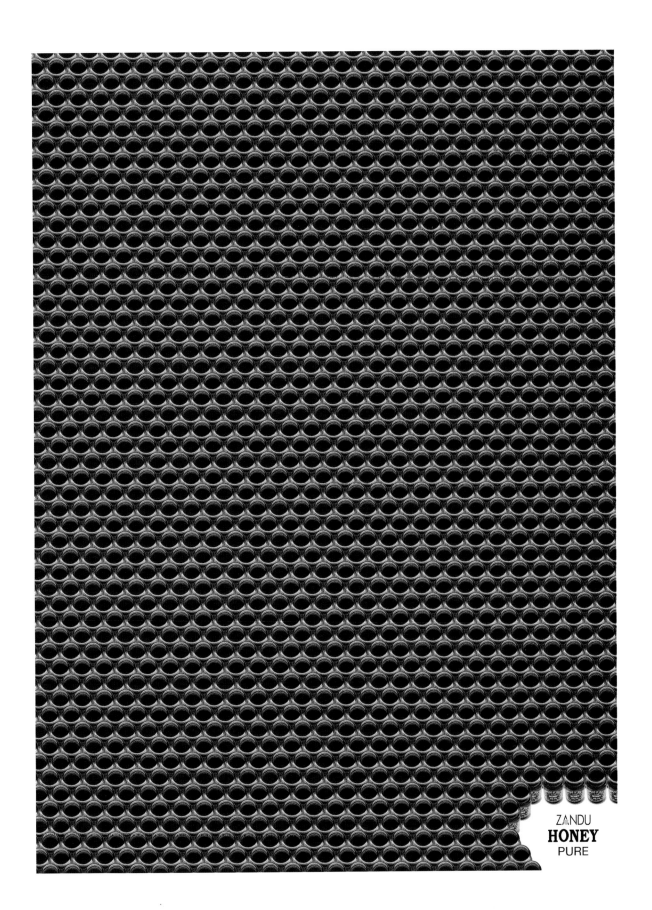

ZANDU
HONEY
PURE

Agency: Saatchi & Saatchi India Creative Directors: Ramesh Ramanathan and Shabnam Sirur Art Director: Ashok Lad Photographer: Vinay Patil Copywriter: Debamgshu Kumar Kerr Client: Zandu Pharmaceutical Works

Have a break.

Have a break.

Have a break.

Creative Director: Tony Granger Art Directors: Suzanne Lynch, David Lloyd and Phillip Squier Photographer: Cleo Sullivan Copywriters: Marc Guttesman, Rob Rooney and Alisa Schindler Group Creative Director: Rich Levy Client: Duncan Hines

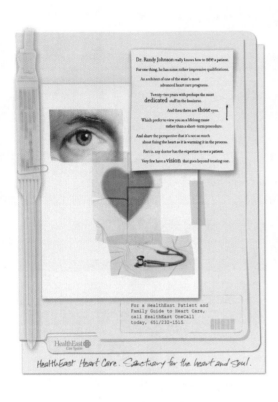

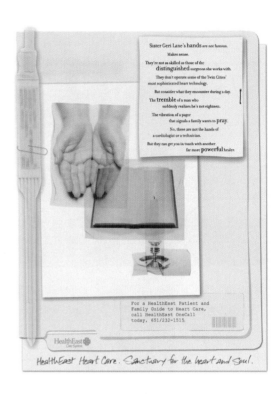

IMPORTANT PIECE OF THE FINNISH HEALTHCARE.

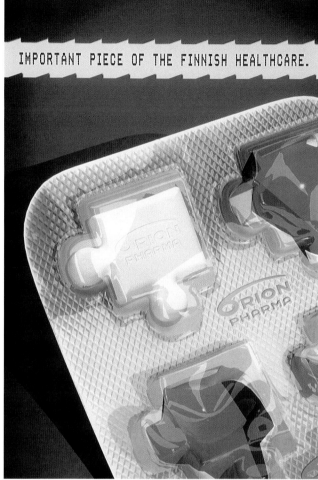

IMPORTANT PIECE OF THE FINNISH HEALTHCARE.

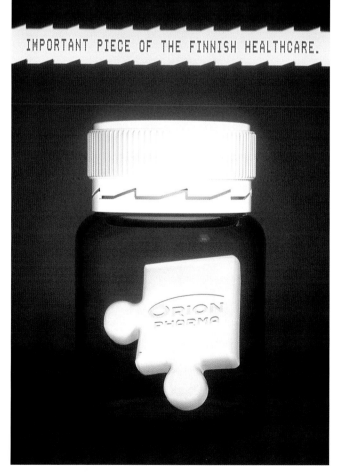

IMPORTANT PIECE OF THE FINNISH HEALTHCARE.

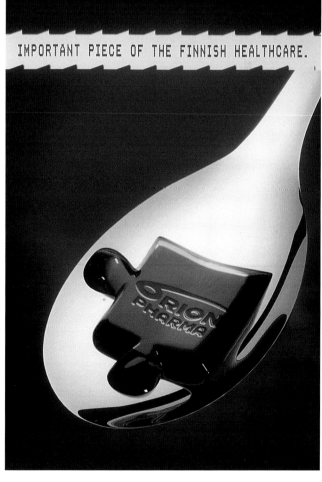

IMPORTANT PIECE OF THE FINNISH HEALTHCARE.

Agency: Tbwa/Phs Creative Directors: Mika Wist and Juha Larsson Art Directors: Mika Wist, Juha Larsson Copywriter: Erkko Mannila Illustrator: Hybrid Oy Copywriter: Erkko Mannila Client: Orion Orion Pharma

Happy Halloween.

You can always tell an Oral-B house. Because an Oral-B toothbrush removes more plaque than any other for healthier teeth and gums. No wonder it's the brand more dentists use themselves.

What kind of
filling
did you get?

Caramel? Nougat? Silver? Make sure you only get the fillings you want.
With an Oral-B® toothbrush. The brand more dentists use themselves.

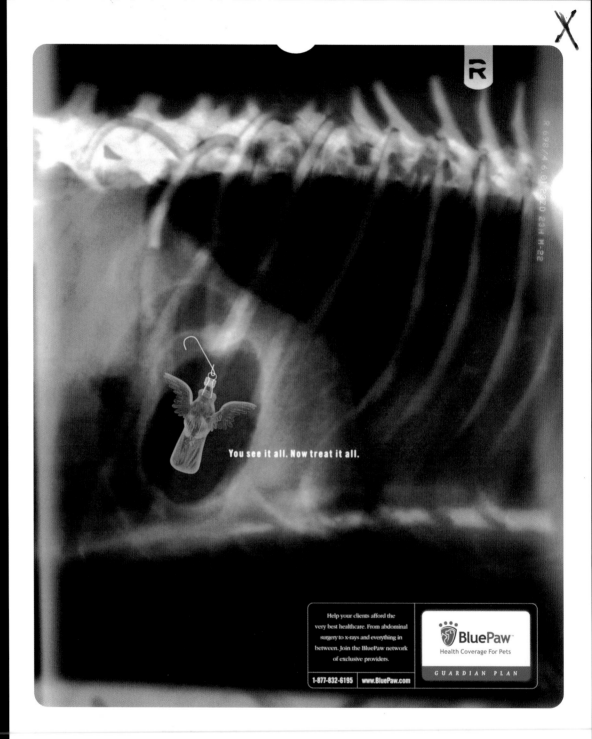

You see it all. Now treat it all.

Help your clients afford the
very best healthcare. From abdominal
surgery to x-rays and everything in
between. Join the BluePaw network
of exclusive providers.

BluePaw
Health Coverage For Pets

GUARDIAN PLAN

1-877-832-6195 | www.BluePaw.com

Insurance
Santander Mexicano

Insurance
Santander Mexicano

We're very, very dedicated to business.

screen employees | generate sales leads | design a website | promote your business | find a corporate lawyer

All Business
www.allbusiness.com

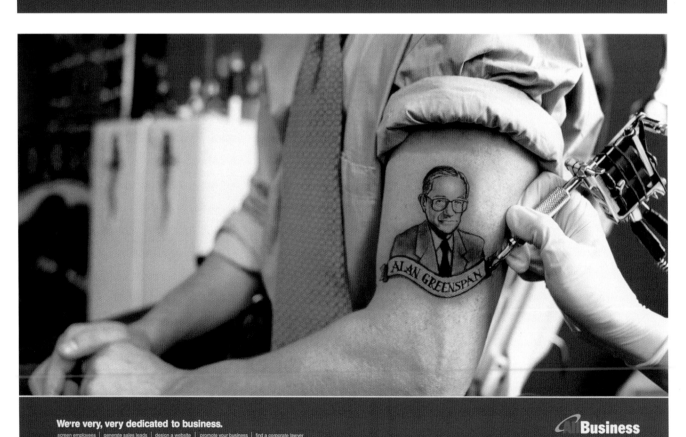

We're very, very dedicated to business.

screen employees | generate sales leads | design a website | promote your business | find a corporate lawyer

All Business
www.allbusiness.com

'Bench' and 'Tattoo' Agency: Butler, Shine & Stern Creative Directors: John Butler and Mike Shine Art Director: Jerome Marucci Designer: Rudi Anggono Photographer: Steve Simmons Copywriter: Sean Austin Client: All Business.com

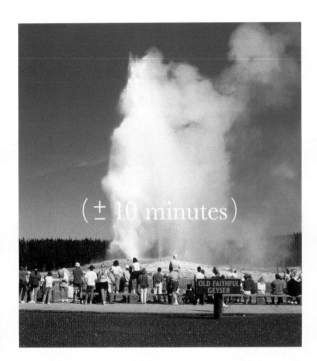

(± 10 minutes)

L O U D C L O U D (±0)

The world is unpredictable. Your Internet operations shouldn't be. Companies like FoxSports.com, adidas and USATODAY.com count on us every day to keep them up and running. How predictable is your infrastructure? Visit www.loudcloud.com/reliable or call 866-259-1550.

LOUDCLOUD

(±1 inch)

L O U D C L O U D (±0)

LOUDCLOUD

Borderfree. We've pledged allegiance to saving you money on the latest electronics online.

Visit us at: excite.ca excite for @ Home

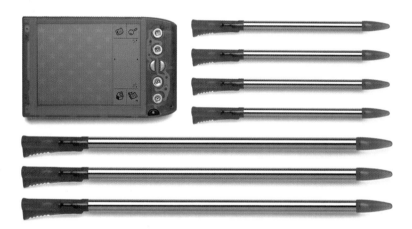

Borderfree. Defending your constitutional right to low-priced gadgets online.

Visit us at: excite.ca excite for @ Home

Borderfree. Dedicated to life, liberty and the pursuit of cool U.S. stuff online.

Visit us at: excite.ca excite for @ Home

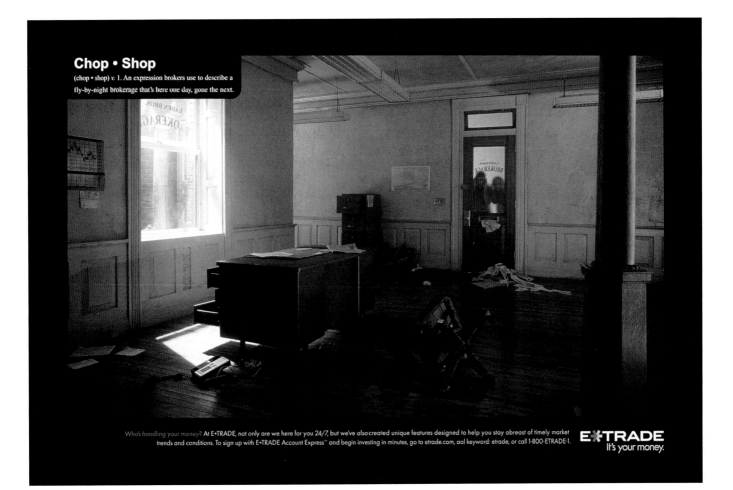

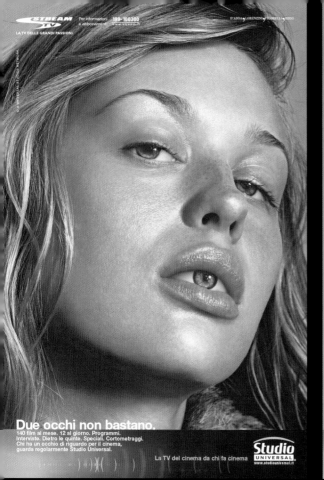

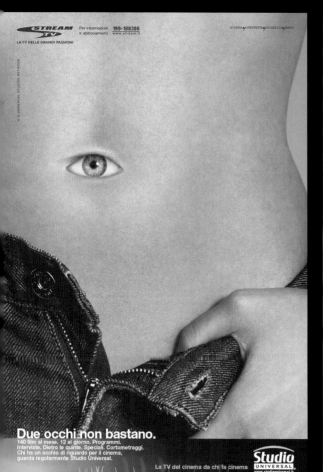
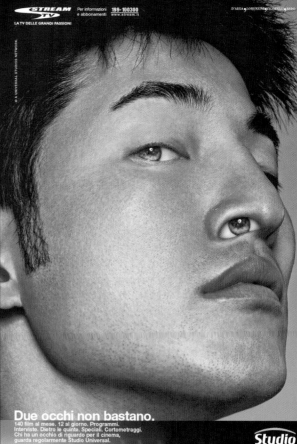

Music TV that's not for kids
vh1co.uk

'Hamster,' 'Hired,' 'Penis' and '15 Minutes' Agency: Taxi Creative Directors: Zak Mroueh and Paul Lavoie Art Director: Rose Sauquillo Copywriter: Jane Murray Client: U8TV

I can name that tune in one note.

The unmistakable sound of a Harley, compliments of these Touring Mufflers with Billet End Caps. See the entire line in the new Genuine Motor Accessories catalog. Pick one up at your H-D dealer. Call 1-800-443-2153 for directions.

Joggers think hard about their shoes. Bikers think hard about their seats and are glad they're not joggers.

The Sundowner™ Touring Bucket Seat. Comfort for long rides. Harley styling to keep it pure. Available for most models. Pick up the latest Genuine Motor Accessories catalog at your H-D dealer. Call 1-800-443-2153 for directions.

The Mona Lisa could've used some flames or an eagle.

Doing our own paint has taught us a thing or two about art. Custom paint from the Harley-Davidson® Color Shop. See the full collection of designs in the new Genuine Motor Accessories catalog. Pick one up at your Harley dealer. 1-800-443-2153.

When is enough chrome enough?
When the kickstand cracks your garage floor.

If you're building a rolling tribute to metal, we can help you nail the look you're going for. The new Genuine Motor Accessories catalog is packed with thousands of eyeball-tickling ideas. Pick up a copy at your Harley-Davidson dealer. Call 1-800-443-2153 for directions.

After bolting on the last piece,
Gary declared that freedom had a new name: Gary.

We've all got one. It's parked in our heads. A dream bike. When you're ready to take it from mind to metal, we've got the parts to create the look you're after. Pick up the new Genuine Motor Accessories catalog at your Harley dealer. Call 1-800-443-2153 for locations.

Customizing. Something to do when you're
not riding thinking about riding. or riding.

There's more to life than your Harley.™ There's also the chrome and leather that go on it. Personalize it from front to tail with authentic H-D custom parts. Pick up the Genuine Motor Accessories catalog at your Harley dealer. Call 1-800-443-2153 for the nearest location.

SOMEWHERE ON AN AIRPLANE A MAN IS TRYING TO RIP OPEN A SMALL BAG OF PEANUTS.

Give us life at ground level, rolling along the endless highway on a Harley-Davidson. 100% depressurized. Just sunlight on chrome. The voice of a V-Twin ripping the open air. And elbow room, stretching all the way to the horizon. Maybe you too think this is the way life ought to be lived. Time to spread some wings. 1-800-443-2153 or www.harley-davidson.com. **The Legend Rolls On.**

MAY ALL YOUR ENCOUNTERS WITH THE LAW START WITH THE WORDS "NICE HARLEY."

Be forewarned. There'll be no keeping a low profile on this one. Raw Sportster muscle, with a look last seen mixing it up at the local dirt track. Orange and black racing paint job. Wide flat-track handlebar. Curvaceous 2-into-1 exhaust. The new Sportster 883R. Lucky thing there's no law against having a little fun. 1-800-443-2153 or www.harley-davidson.com. **The Legend Rolls On.**

NO. I'VE DECIDED TO OPT FOR A SMALL AND RATHER UNEVENTFUL LIFE.

You could eat up a lifetime pondering what to do with your days on earth. Or you could take one look at a machine like the Wide Glide. And let gut instinct take it from there. Get a load of the high handlebar and stretched-out profile. We didn't hold anything back in building this ride. So what's holding you back? 1-800-443-2153 or www.harley-davidson.com. **The Legend Rolls On.**

Agency: Martin/Williams, Inc. Creative Directors: Jim Henderson and Tom Kelly Art Director: Bryan Michurski Photographer: Chris Michurski Copywriter: Chris Sheehan Retoucher: Lyle Wedemeyer Retoucher: Chris Sheehan Client: Victory Motorcycles

Motorcycles 124, 125

'Mike Cascone,' 'Mike Uno' and 'Buster Fought'

GOING UP IN A ROCKET ISN'T NEARLY AS COURAGEOUS AS SITTING IN FRONT OF ONE.

THE MOTOR SPORTS HALL OF FAME enshrines the heroes of horsepower on land, on water and in the air. Visit us in Novi, Michigan and at www.mshf.com. Or call 1.800.250.RACE.

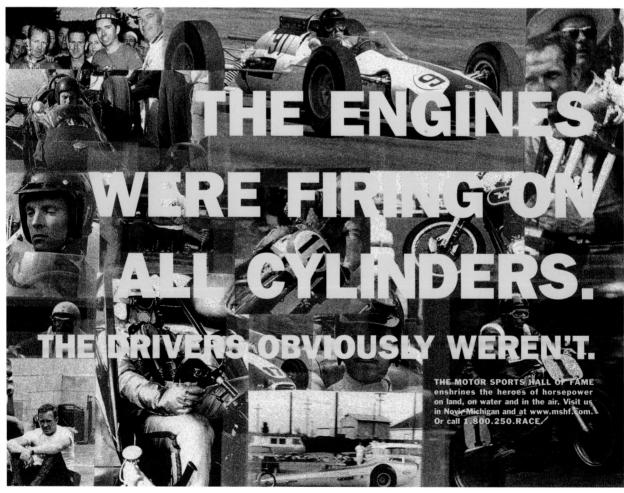

THE ENGINES WERE FIRING ON ALL CYLINDERS. THE DRIVERS OBVIOUSLY WEREN'T.

THE MOTOR SPORTS HALL OF FAME enshrines the heroes of horsepower on land, on water and in the air. Visit us in Novi, Michigan and at www.mshf.com. Or call 1.800.250.RACE.

The Richards Group Creative Director: Glen Dady Art Director: Jimmy Bonner Photographer: Rob Baker Client: Age of Steam Railroad Museum Copywriter: Andy Bennett

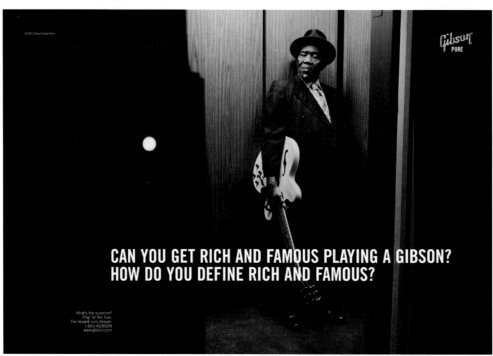

Your birth marked the new era. Happy 20th Anniversary.

Sony Music Entertainment Inc.

'MTV 20th Anniversary' Agency: Sony Music Entertainment Art Director: Ria Shibayama Illustrator: Ria Shibayama Copywriter: David Lanfain Client: Sony Music Entertainment

WHEN YOU USE HI WHITE , IT SHOWS.

When you feel the heat, it's working.

BENGAY
GREASELESS PAIN RELIEVING CREAM
FOR MINOR ARTHRITIS, BACKACHE, MUSCLE & JOINT PAIN

'Pop Corn' Agency: Circulo Lowe Lintas Creative Director: Norma Jean Colberg Art Directors: Francisco Fernandez and Victor Lleras

Designers: Victor Lleras and Francisco Fernandez Photographers: Francisco Fernandez and Clay Humphrey Copywriters: Victor Lleras and Francisco Fernandez Account Coordiators: Victor Lleras and Francisco Ferndez Client: Pfizer · Pharmaceuticals 132, 133

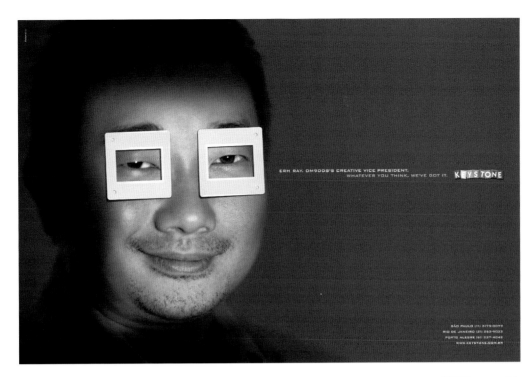

ERH RAY, DM9DDB'S CREATIVE VICE PRESIDENT.
WHATEVER YOU THINK, WE'VE GOT IT. **KEYSTONE**

SÃO PAULO (11) 3179-0079
RIO DE JANEIRO (21) 253-9033
PORTO ALEGRE (51) 337-4042
WWW.KEYSTONE.COM.BR

KEYSTONE TOMÁS LORENTE, AGE'S CREATIVE DIRECTOR.
WHATEVER YOU THINK, WE'VE GOT IT.

SÃO PAULO (11) 3179-0079
RIO DE JANEIRO (21) 253-9033
PORTO ALEGRE (51) 337-4042
WWW.KEYSTONE.COM.BR

JAVIER TALAVERA, DPZ'S CREATIVE DIRECTOR.
WHATEVER YOU THINK, WE'VE GOT IT. **KEYSTONE**

SÃO PAULO (11) 3179-0079
RIO DE JANEIRO (21) 253-9033
PORTO ALEGRE (51) 337-4042
WWW.KEYSTONE.COM.BR

'Whatever you think, we've got it' Agency: Fischer Amércia Creative Director: Paulo Pretti Art Director: Paulo Pretti Creative Director: Paulo Pretti Account Coordinator: Paulo Pretti Copywriter: Paulo Pretti Photographer: Claudio Elisabetsky Client: Keystone

Air Fantaposite. We would like to take this opportunity to thank the waffle maker and dogs that chase cars. The three a.m. kung-fu movie, Murphy for the law, a free ride, it's and it is. The hill, the road, the pitch, the path, the track and the pizza delivery guy. Knowing how to compensate. All the Greek gods, rollercoasters and the wake up call. What you know, what you don't know and everyone that ever asked why. For and against. High tide, noodles and the smell of wet grass. The lightweight, the heavyweight, extremes and everything in the middle that made it possible. Arrogance, the attitude problem and the tooth fairy. Darwin and tying your own shoe laces. Who you are, not who you were. The human beat-box, spray paint, the train and just a bit further. Grinning like a fool and wearing nothing but a smile. Whoever thought of subtitles, mushrooms, **gold teeth**, ninjas and museums. Something from nothing, all that you've got, not a lot being too much and Joan of Arc. The 24hr video store, those willing to talk about it and **for**tune cookies. Anyone that walked on the wild side, never and ever. The letter, the word and freedom to say f**k it all. Stairs, the lift, the taxi and anyone that made it to the end. The remote control, lounging, the shopping channel, how and why. That girl on the bus this morning, the glance, the look and the stare. An attempt, the failure and caring without giving a damn. Your best and **your** worst. The ego, the id, keeping the faith, losing your mind and king size. Remembering that you haven't seen it all before. Deodorant, the excuse, planet Earth and the first person to look at the stars. Vending machines, supermarkets and fruit trees. The stop sign and the day off. Certain animals (you know who you are). Inventor of the ball, hoop, bat, club, stick, cue and duvet. The running man, woman, **feet** and wherever it is you're going anyway. Keeping it real, truth, the warp drive, days when it rains frogs and dreaming you can fly. Whoever wrote the rules, anyone that broke the rules and anyone or anything else that has ever inspired us.

Agency: Wieden + Kennedy, Amsterdam Creative Directors: Glenn Cole and Paul Shearer Art Director: Robert Nakata Designer: Robert Nakata Photographer: Toby McFarland Pond Copywriter: Richard Gorodecky Account Coordinator: Gemma Requesens Client: Nike

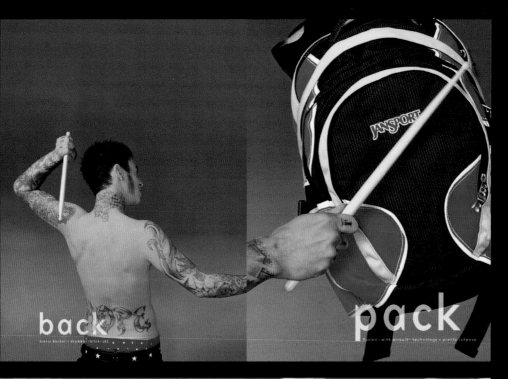

'Travis Barker,' 'Pink' and 'Jessica Alba' Agency: DDB Seattle

Creative Director: Laurie Fritts Art Director: Shari Layman Designer: Todd Hofmeister Photographer: Cathrine Ledner Copywriter: Laurie Fritts Account Coordinator: Hillary Miller Traffic Director: Robyn Hallonquist Client: JanSport

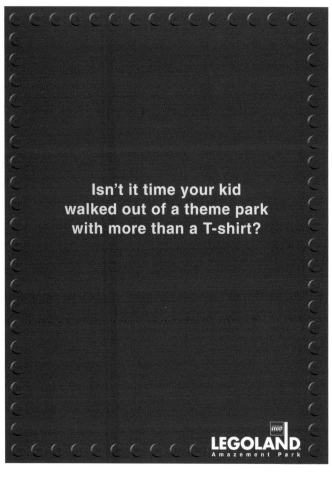

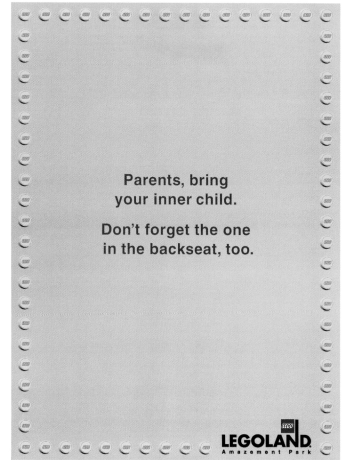

Before you decide
if your kid is right or left-brained,
give both sides a workout.

LEGOLAND.
Amazement

The Power of the Brick.

The Power of the Brick.

The Power of the Brick.

'Temple,' 'Brooklyn Bridge,' 'Great Wall' and 'Sphinx' Agency: Lowe Creative Directors: Gary Goldsmith, Dean Hacohen, Gordon Bennett and Bruce Hopman Art Director: Elizabeth Maertens Copywriter: David Olsen Account Coordinator: Steve McCall Client: Lego

The Power of the Brick.

Steelcase

Steelcase

Can a chair make you
rethink your wardrobe?

'Red Chair' and 'Trashcan' Agency: Martin/Williams, Inc. Creative Director: Tom Kelly Art Director: Tim Tone Photographer: Tim Tone Photographer: Mark Laita Copywriter: Jan Pettit Retoucher: Brad Palm Client: Steelcase

Furniture designed
to make you think better.

A built-in trash can
in case you don't.

Steelcase

The Leap® Chair Coach® Edition / Call your authorized Steelcase dealer or 800.333.9939 / www.steelcase.com

Ergonomic chic.

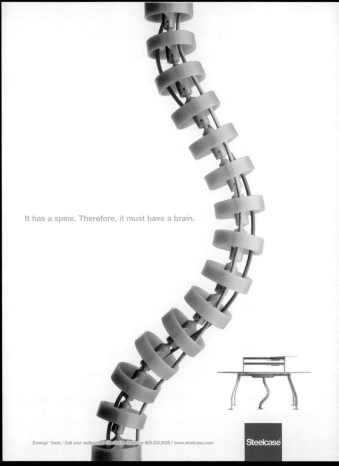

It has a spine. Therefore, it must have a brain.

Emerge™ Desk / Call your authorized Steelcase dealer or 800.333.9939 / www.steelcase.com

Steelcase

Pity you sit

with your back to it.

Reminiscence toilet by American Standard. Another example of how we're bringing an exciting new world of design options to you.

For more proof, visit www.americanstandard-us.com or call 1.800.524.9797, Ext. 200. | *American Standard*

Filthy?

Rich?

Lagaro Bathtub by Porcher. Another example of how we're bringing an exciting new world of design options to you.

For more proof, visit www.porcher-us.com or call 1.800.524.9797, Ext. 200. | PORCHER

Water droplets struggle

not to let go.

Iperbole by Porcher. Another example of how we're bringing an exciting new world of design options to you.

For more proof, visit www.americanstandard-us.com or call 1.800.524.9797, Ext. 200. | PORCHER

Stare at it long enough

and it starts

to look like a sink.

Como Basin by Porcher. Another example of how we're bringing an exciting new world of design options to you.

For more proof, visit www.porcher-us.com or call 1.800.524.9797, Ext. 200.

PORCHER
for *American Standard*

It's your world.

Live better.

This is what happens when pen designers are given unlimited access to espresso.

The Pen, Pushed. CROSS.

INTRODUCING **ION**™ PURE ENERGY AND FUN IN A PALM-SIZED DESIGN. THERE'S A SOFT-TOUCH GRIP, "QUICK-CLIP" ATTACHMENT AND SIX VIBRANT GEL INK COLORS. ADD IN A LIFETIME MECHANICAL WARRANTY, AND IT'S CREATIVITY AT ITS FINEST. SEE IT AT A RETAILER OR **CROSS.COM**.

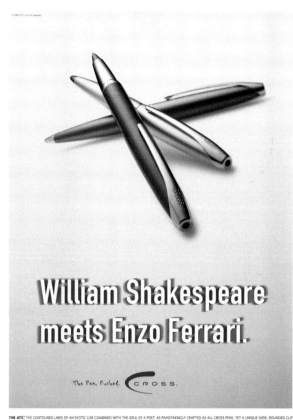

William Shakespeare meets Enzo Ferrari.

The Pen, Pushed. CROSS.

THE ATX™ THE CONTOURED LINES OF AN EXOTIC CAR COMBINED WITH THE SOUL OF A POET. AS PAINSTAKINGLY CRAFTED AS ALL CROSS PENS, YET A UNIQUE WIDE, ROUNDED CLIP GIVES IT A LOOK LIKE NO OTHER. CHOOSE FROM FOUR DIFFERENT WRITING TECHNOLOGIES, EACH COVERED BY A LIFETIME MECHANICAL WARRANTY. SEE THEM AT **CROSS.COM**.

SHOWN: THE 10-KARAT GOLD-FILLED CLASSIC™ CENTURY™ BALLPOINT AND MEDALIST™ CLASSIC™ CENTURY™ BALLPOINT PENS.

Ink. Beautifully gift-wrapped in 10-karat gold.

The Pen, Pushed. CROSS.

GIVE A GIFT AS TIMELESS AS THE ACT OF GIVING ITSELF. THE **CROSS CLASSIC**™ **CENTURY**™ PERFECTLY BALANCED FOR A REFINED FEEL. GOLD-FILLED TO MAKE SUCH FEELINGS JUSTIFIED. A LIFETIME MECHANICAL WARRANTY HELPS ENSURE THEY'LL KEEP IT FOR YEARS TO COME. SEE IT AT **CROSS.COM**.

Eliminates writer's cramp. For writer's block, try tequila.

The Pen, Pushed. CROSS.

THE MORPH.™ SO COMFORTABLE, YOU'LL WRITE 'TIL YOU HIT THE WORM. THE ADJUSTABLE SILICONE GRIP MOLDS TO THE HAND. A COOL FLOATING BALL CLIP GLIDES INTO POCKETS. A LIFETIME MECHANICAL WARRANTY MEANS IT'LL GO AS LONG AS YOU. SEE IT AT A RETAILER OR **CROSS.COM**.

'Espresso,' 'Shakespeare,' 'Ink' and 'Writer's Block' Agency: Carmichael Lynch Creative Director: Jim Nelson Art Director: Jeff Terwilliger Copywriter: Conn Newton Account Coordinator: Dan Mandle Client: A.T. Cross

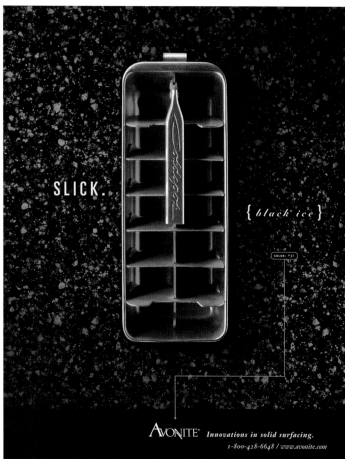

Ein ganzer Kerl dank Chappi®

Lunar Design

www.lunar.com

541 Eighth Street San Francisco, CA 94103 415) 252–4388
537 Hamilton Avenue Palo Alto, CA 94301 650) 326–7788

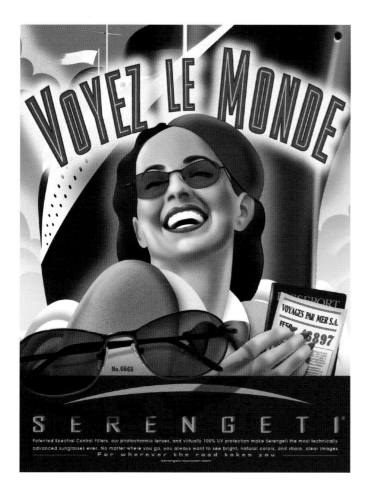

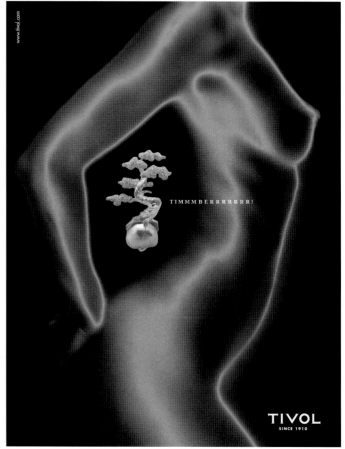

TRUSTED TO PROTECT A SYMBOL OF OUR FREEDOM.

INCLUDING THE RIGHT TO SPEND LESS TIME IN THE KITCHEN.

While Teflon® is helping preserve the Statue of Liberty, our new Teflon® non-stick coatings are helping make your life easier. Breakthrough innovations like our "Life-Proof" DuPont™ Teflon® Platinum provides extraordinary abrasion and scratch resistance, making cookware even more durable against life's challenges. It's a whole new generation of Teflon® for a whole new generation of cooks. Visit Teflon.com.

Life made smoother.

IF IT CAN HOLD UP AGAINST THE RIGORS OF SPACE.

HOW BAD CAN A SPATULA BE?

Teflon® innovations have helped ease the stress on the Space Shuttle, while our new Teflon® non-stick coatings are easing the stress life puts on your cookware. For example, there's our "Life-Proof" Teflon® Platinum, with its extraordinary abrasion and scratch resistance surface, so your cookware can work and look new even longer. Hey, if DuPont™ Teflon® is durable enough for space travel, it can surely survive a cooking mishap. Visit Teflon.com.

Life made smoother.

WE'VE HELPED PUT A MAN ON THE MOON.

AND A BETTER OMELET ON YOUR BREAKFAST TABLE.

Not only are we part of the great discoveries in space, our new achievements in the kitchen are pretty remarkable as well. Like new DuPont™ Teflon® Platinum non-stick coating- it's so revolutionary, we call it "Life-Proof," with its extraordinary abrasion and scratch resistance surface. Thanks to Teflon® Platinum and all the new Teflon® coatings, life here on earth will be that much easier. Visit Teflon.com.

Life made smoother.

MONO

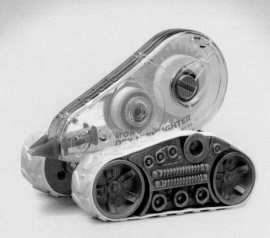

///// **Highlight important thoughts on just about any surface.** /////

u nlike liquid highlighters, the MONO® Dry Highlighter works on all kinds of papers – glossy, thermal, super-thin, you name it. With no bleeding or drying time. You get a clean, precise line that's erasable. It's the smart choice for highlighting your thoughts. Wherever they may lead.

800-835-3232 | Lawrenceville, GA | tombowusa.com

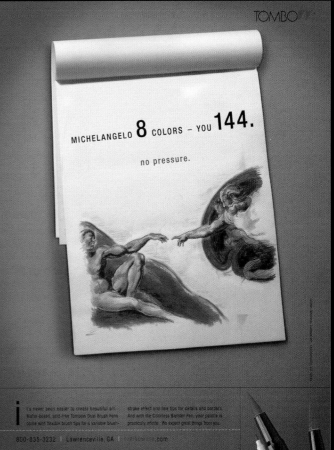

TOMBOW

MICHELANGELO **8** COLORS – YOU **144.**

no pressure.

i t's never been easier to create beautiful art. Water-based, acid-free Tombow Dual Brush Pens come with flexible brush tips for a variable brush-stroke effect and fine line tips for details and borders. And with the Colorless Blender Pen, your palette is practically infinite. We expect great things from you.

800-835-3232 | Lawrenceville, GA | tombowusa.com

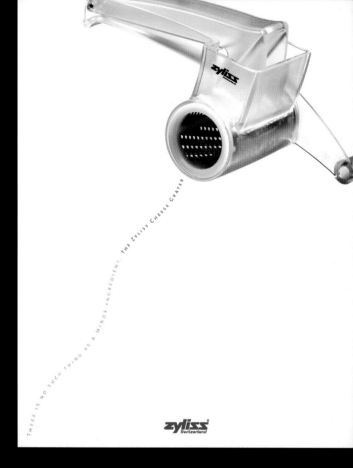

A MASTER CHEF DOESN'T TRY

TO ENHANCE AN INGREDIENT,

BUT EXTRACTS ITS ESSENCE.

THE ZYLISS GARLIC PRESS

zyliss
Switzerland

THERE IS NO SUCH THING AS A MINOR INGREDIENT: THE ZYLISS CHEESE GRATER

zyliss
Switzerland

'Digital Proofs to Live By' Agency: Mullen Creative Directors: Michael Ancevic; Edward Boches and Stephen Mietelski Art Director: Michael Ancevic Photographer: Moshe Braka Copywriters: Craig Walker and Stephen Mietelski Account Coordinator: Don Lorenzet Client: AGFA Products: 164.165

IT'S TWICE THE MACHINE IT USED TO BE. WITH HALF THE PARTS.

The Ultra-Reliable XLi. *Further proof Trane has a comfortable lead.*

We put a lot of thought into the new Trane XLi. So much thought, in fact, that we had to make room for it all. So we designed our XLi unit to function with half the parts. That means easier installation and enhanced service access—access you'll likely never need, thanks to the unit's improved reliability. We topped things off with a sleek new roof and a new noncorrosive basepan, then backed it all with the best limited warranty out there: ten years on the compressor, outdoor coil and internal functional parts. Our ultimate goal? To deliver a product that doubles your sales—in half the time.

TRANE
It's Hard To Stop A Trane.
www.trane.com

GENIUS IS 1% INSPIRATION AND 99% PERSPIRATION. WELL, IT WAS.

The XL 1800 Ultra Efficiency Air Conditioner. *Further proof Trane has a comfortable lead.*

Thousands of hours spent sweating the small stuff. That's what goes into each XL 1800, in addition to twin Climatuff™ compressors and innovations like Comfort-R™ airflow. The result of this obsessive attention to detail? A comfort system that reaches 18 SEER. Translate that into customer-speak and you're talking greater energy efficiency, lower operating costs, improved humidity control and quieter operation. In other words, one very smart buy.

TRANE
It's Hard To Stop A Trane.
www.trane.com

THINKING OUTSIDE OF THE BOX LED TO FINDING A QUICK WAY BACK IN.

The Easy-Access Comfort Coil. *Further proof Trane has a comfortable lead.*

It's easy to see why our Comfort Coil has been hailed as a true innovation. Its access door and split front panels make everything easy to see, from the foil insulation to the coil fins. Easy to see means easy to clean, which in turn means greater efficiency and lower maintenance costs. In addition, the coil cabinet fits our furnaces without any forced "adjustments," while a two-way sloped drain pan improves indoor air quality. The end result of these enhancements? You'll see greater sales.

TRANE
It's Hard To Stop A Trane.
www.trane.com

'Diamonds' Agency: Cole & Weber/Red Cell Creative Directors: Guy Seese and Dave Cook Art Directors: Dan Lucey and Tana Kosiyabong Photographer: Fritz Kok Copywriters: Michael Ludwig, Andrew Ure and Ann Mason Account Coordinator: Janique Helson Client: Haribo Gummi Bears

www.duncanyoyo.com

★★ SO AUTHENTIC ★★

it will make a tiny plastic FRENCHMAN

start waving his 1/35 scale

WHITE FLAG.

[GERMAN TIGER 1 INITIAL PRODUCTION. 1/35 SCALE.]

ONE OF THE MOST FEARSOME TANKS EVER TO ROLL ONTO A BATTLEFIELD. The Tiger I Initial Production first saw action in the African Theatre under Rommel, and later came to be feared in Europe and on the Russian front as well. Tamiya has recreated this formidable fighting machine right down to the smallest detail. Including many features that distinguish the initial production model from later versions. The result is a truly convincing replica of this intimidating armored vehicle. Especially so, to the residents of a scaled-down occupied country.

[Learn more at www.tamiya.com or 1-800-5TAMIYA]

TAMIYA

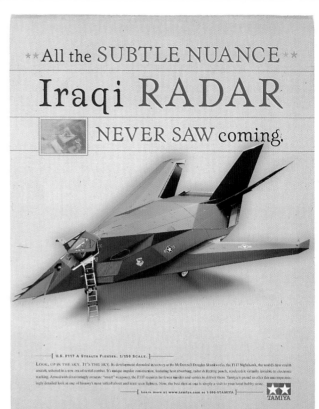

★★ All the SUBTLE NUANCE ★★

Iraqi RADAR

NEVER SAW coming.

[U.S. F117 A STEALTH FIGHTER. 1/150 SCALE.]

LOOK, UP IN THE SKY. IT'S THE SKY. In development shrouded in secrecy at the McDonnell Douglas Skunkworks, the F117 Nighthawk, the world's first stealth aircraft, ushered in a new era of aerial combat. Its unique angular construction, featuring heat-absorbing, radar deflecting panels, rendered it virtually invisible to electronic tracking. Armed with devastatingly accurate "smart" weaponry, the F117 requires far fewer missiles and sorties to deliver them. Tamiya is proud to offer this uncompromisingly detailed look at one of history's most talked about and least seen fighters. Now, the best shot at one is simply a visit to your local hobby store.

[Learn more at www.tamiya.com or 1-800-5TAMIYA]

TAMIYA

EVERYONE HAS BREAD BUT NOT EVERYONE HAS A PORSCHE.

SIEMENS

Presenting a toaster designed by Porsche.

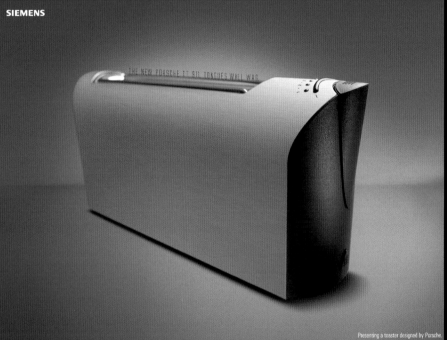

THE NEW PORSCHE TT 911. TONGUES WILL WAG.

Presenting a toaster designed by Porsche.

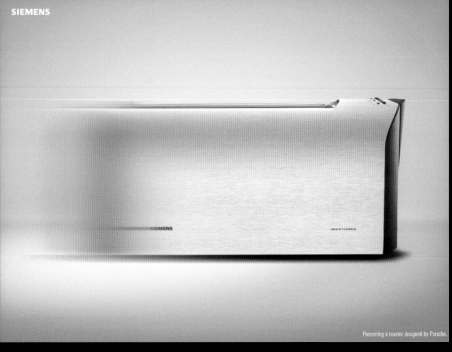

SIEMENS

Presenting a toaster designed by Porsche.

Creative Director: Sanjay Sipahimalani Art Director: Juiu Basu Designer: Juiu Basu Photographer: Raj Mistray Illustrator: Sanjay Shetye Copywriter: Randip De Account Coordinator: Sushant Panda Client: BSH Home Appliances   Products: 170

'Michael Jackson,' 'Bread,' 'Tongues Wag' and 'Speed' Agency: Grey Worldwide (I) PVT, Ltd.

Suggested wine:
Argyle '96 Brut.
Ripe pear and toast
aroma. Flavors of
apple and vanilla.
Serve well chilled.

eVineyard

Over 5000 wines. Savvy advice from people who know wine. Gifts and accessories. eVineyard.com

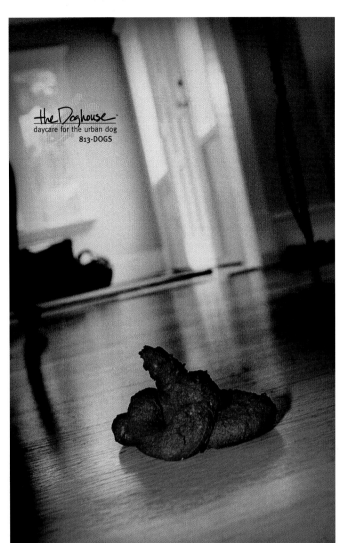

(this page) Agency: Young & Rubicam Vancouver Creative Directors: Kevin Barclay and Don Veinish Photographer: Brad Stringer Copywriter: Don Veinish Client: The Doghouse   Products 172,173

Sanders, Lyn & Ragonetti Associates, Trial Lawyers

202-195 County Court Blvd. Brampton, Ontario L6W-4P7 Tel:(905)450-1711 Fax:(905)450-7066 www.slra.com

Sanders, Lyn & Ragonetti Associates, Trial Lawyers

202-195 County Court Blvd. Brampton, Ontario L6W-4P7 Tel:(905)450-1711 Fax:(905)450-7066 www.slra.com

FischerAmérica 18 unexpected years.

178 Unexpected Years' Agency: Fischer América Creative Director: Paulo Pretti Art Directors: Paulo Pretti and Daniel Venticinque Photographer: Ricardo de Vicq Copywriters: Sérgio Scarpelli and Edgard Gianesi Account Coordinator: Eduardo Fischer Client: Fischer América

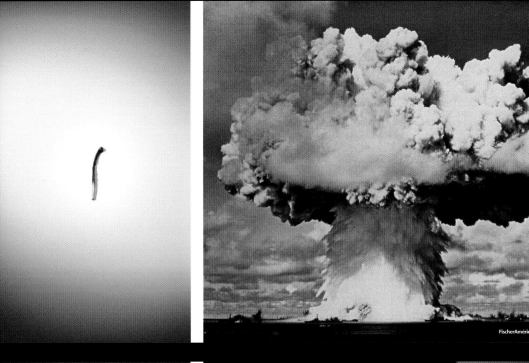

Mac supporter wanted.

Jung von Matt/Limmat, Wolfbachstrasse 19, 8032 Zürich, Telefon 01 254 66 00, www.jvm.ch

JUNG v. MATT
an der Limmat

STEVEN STANKIEWICZ **TECHNICAL ILLUSTRATOR** 212.477.4229

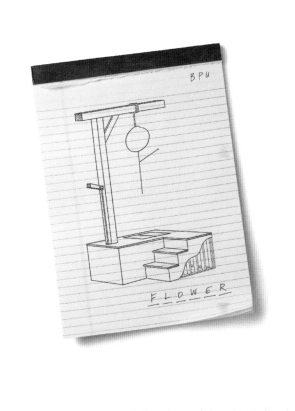

STEVEN STANKIEWICZ **TECHNICAL ILLUSTRATOR** 212.477.4229

Agency: Butler, Shine & Stern Creative Director: John Butler Art Director: Jerry Underwood Photographer: Brian Mahany Illustrator: Steven Stankiewicz Copywriter: Alex Grossman Client: Steven Stankiewicz, Illustrator Professional Services

'Etch-a-Sketch' and 'Hang Man'

WE'RE YOUNG.
BUT WE'RE OLD ENOUGH TO KNOW WHAT CRAP IS.

Steele Films produces award winning commercials for Pytka's lunch money.

www.steelefilms.com
310.581.5354

DAVID STONE FREELANCE COPYWRITER 303-438-1621

©2001 Gold's Gym

Spare Tire Removal

For more info, call or come by any of our Columbia area locations.

508 Evelyn Dr   275-2 Harbison Blvd   9940 Two Notch Rd #108   619 N Lake Dr
803-798-1000   803-749-9700   803-419-0222   803-359-6100

GOLD'S GYM

©2001 Gold's Gym

©2001 Gold's Gym

Lean Calves Available

Small Ass For Sale

For more info, call or come by any of our Columbia area locations.

508 Evelyn Dr	275-2 Harbison Blvd	9940 Two Notch Rd #108	619 N Lake Dr
803-798-1000	803-749-9700	803-419-0222	803-359-6100

For more info, call or come by any of our Columbia area locations.

508 Evelyn Dr	275-2 Harbison Blvd	9940 Two Notch Rd #108	619 N Lake Dr
803-798-1000	803-749-9700	803-419-0222	803-359-6100

Professional

How to become the King of (insert your product here).

Advertising. The way great brands get to be great brands."

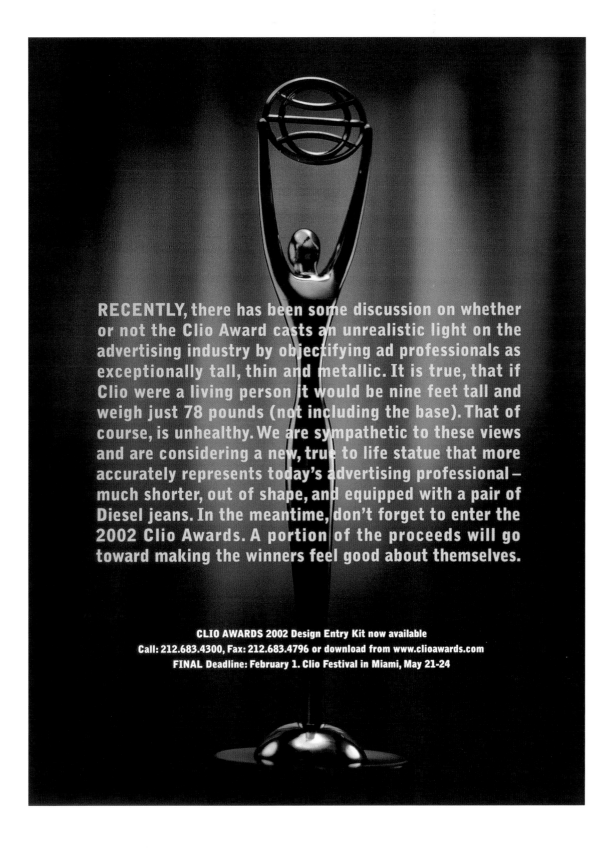

RECENTLY, there has been some discussion on whether or not the Clio Award casts an unrealistic light on the advertising industry by objectifying ad professionals as exceptionally tall, thin and metallic. It is true, that if Clio were a living person it would be nine feet tall and weigh just 78 pounds (not including the base). That of course, is unhealthy. We are sympathetic to these views and are considering a new, true to life statue that more accurately represents today's advertising professional— much shorter, out of shape, and equipped with a pair of Diesel jeans. In the meantime, don't forget to enter the 2002 Clio Awards. A portion of the proceeds will go toward making the winners feel good about themselves.

CLIO AWARDS 2002 Design Entry Kit now available
Call: 212.683.4300, Fax: 212.683.4796 or download from www.clioawards.com
FINAL Deadline: February 1. Clio Festival in Miami, May 21-24

Professional Services 184, 185

Art Director: Steve Sandstrom Designer: Steve Sandstrom Photographer: Steve Sandstrom Copywriter: Jim Haven Production Designer: John Bohls Account Coordinator: Kirsten Cassidy Client: Clio Awards

Agency: Sandstrom Design Creative Director: Steve Sandstrom ◀

GET THERE.

EILAKAISLA
PRIVATE PERSONNEL AGENCY

GET THERE.

EILAKAISLA
PRIVATE PERSONNEL AGENCY

Agency: TBWA/PHS Creative Directors: Samuli Harjunpaa and Mira Leppanen Art Director: Samuli Harjunpaa Photographer: Lasse Karkkainen Copywriter: Mira Leppanen Client: Eilakaisla Recruitment Agency

'Foot in the Door'

'Ripe Old Age,' 'Oral Hygiene' and 'Tell a Story' Agency: Bradley and Montgomery Creative Directors: Mark Bradley and Scott Montgomery Designers: Mark Bradley and Scott Montgomery Client: Sunnyside Dental

LIVING TO A RIPE OLD AGE
IS A LOT MORE FUN
WITH YOUR ORIGINAL TEETH.

Gingivitis	1	17	A lifetime of soda pop
Baseball in the mouth	2	18	Cracked in two after a chewy Spree
Too much pie	3	19	Started to feel funny, then pop
Didn't brush as often as I should have	4	20	Darn near swallowed this one
Got wiggly all of a sudden	5	21	Filling fell out, then forgot about it
Too hard to floss back there	6	22	Mmmmm –Taffy
Even harder to floss there	7	23	Halloween 1977
Toothbrush didn't really fit back there	8	24	Halloween 1976
Penchant for Baby Ruth bars	9	25	Halloween 1975
Took that one for granted	10	26	Actually came out in the carmel
Too sleepy to brush some nights	11	27	Put off dental appointments
Too hurried to brush some mornings	12	28	Didn't heed dental direct mail piece
Who brushes after lunch?	13	29	Easter 1974
Came out after #13	14	30	Easter 1973
Came out after #14	15	31	Easter 1972
I like to chew on ice	16	32	It was in the way of the dentures

TAKE GOOD CARE OF YOUR TEETH. SEE US AND BE SURE YOU ARE.

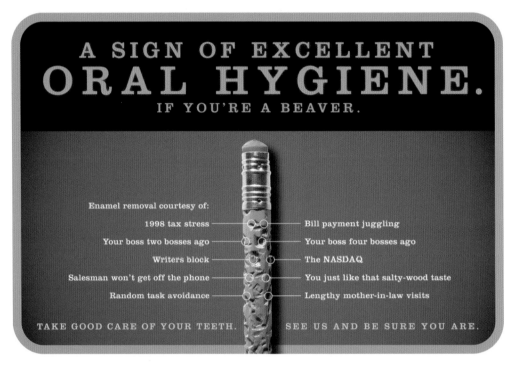

A SIGN OF EXCELLENT
ORAL HYGIENE.
IF YOU'RE A BEAVER.

Enamel removal courtesy of:

1998 tax stress	Bill payment juggling
Your boss two bosses ago	Your boss four bosses ago
Writers block	The NASDAQ
Salesman won't get off the phone	You just like that salty-wood taste
Random task avoidance	Lengthy mother-in-law visits

TAKE GOOD CARE OF YOUR TEETH. SEE US AND BE SURE YOU ARE.

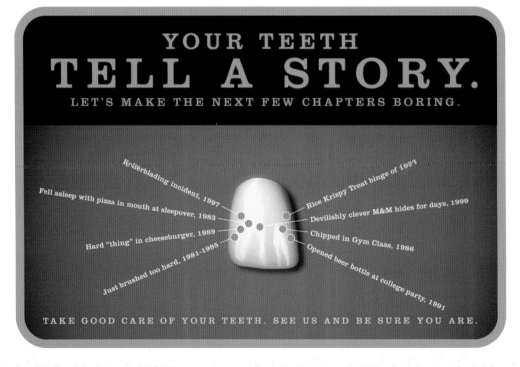

YOUR TEETH
TELL A STORY.
LET'S MAKE THE NEXT FEW CHAPTERS BORING.

Rollerblading incident, 1997
Fell asleep with pizza in mouth at sleepover, 1983
Hard "thing" in cheeseburger, 1989
Just brushed too hard, 1981-1995
Rice Krispy Treat binge of 1993
Devilishly clever M&M hides for days, 1999
Chipped in Gym Class, 1986
Opened beer bottle at college party, 1991

TAKE GOOD CARE OF YOUR TEETH. SEE US AND BE SURE YOU ARE.

SIMPL®

CUT PRICES

by Mic Hairstyling

Agency: Arih Advertising Agency Creative Director: Igor Arih Art Director: Slavimir Stojanovic Designer: Slavimir Stojanovic Copywriter: Gal Erbeznik Account Coordinator: Sasa Deu Client: Mitstyling Professional Services 188,189

TAKE YOUR CHILDREN TO WORK DAY
LOWE LINTAS & PARTNERS, THURSDAY, APRIL 26

REALLY TOUGH JUDGING. THE 2002 MARKETING AWARDS.
Entry deadline Dec. 7th. www.marketingmag.ca or call 1-877-301-9590 / 416-596-3569.

REALLY TOUGH JUDGING. THE 2002 MARKETING AWARDS.
Entry deadline Dec. 7th. www.marketingmag.ca or call 1-877-301-9590 / 416-596-3569.

REALLY TOUGH JUDGING. THE 2002 MARKETING AWARDS.
Entry deadline Dec. 7th. www.marketingmag.ca or call 1-877-301-9590 / 416-596-3569.

REALLY TOUGH JUDGING. THE 2002 MARKETING AWARDS.
Entry deadline Dec. 7th. www.marketingmag.ca or call 1-877-301-9590 / 416-596-3569.

'Merit,' 'Hack,' 'Poor Execution' and 'Seen It' Agency: Taxi Creative Directors: Zak Mroueh and Paul Lavoie Art Director: Lance Martin Photographer: Shin Sugino Copywriter: Micheal Mayes Client: Marketing Awards   Professional Services 190,191

¹/₁   *"River without chemical run-off."*

¹/₁   *"River without contaminated fish."*

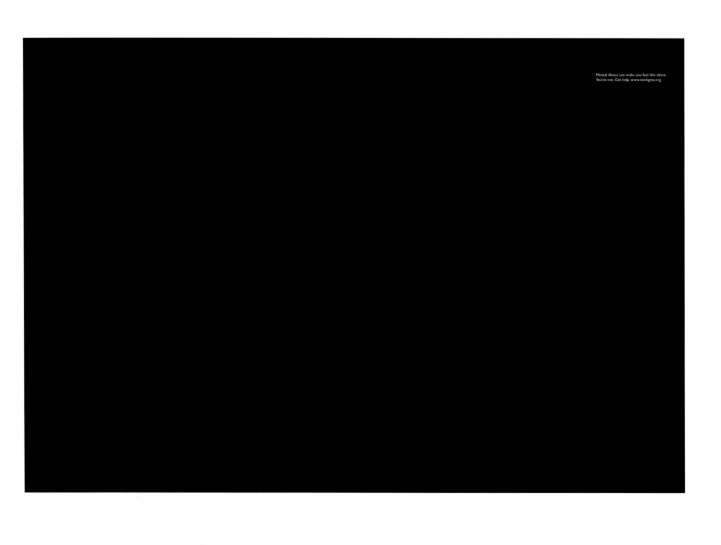

Mental illness can make you feel this alone.
You're not. Get help. www.nostigma.org

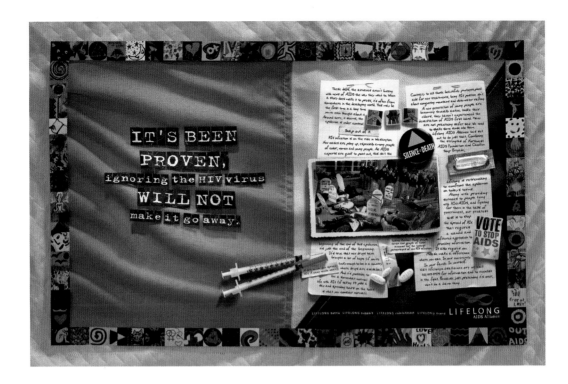

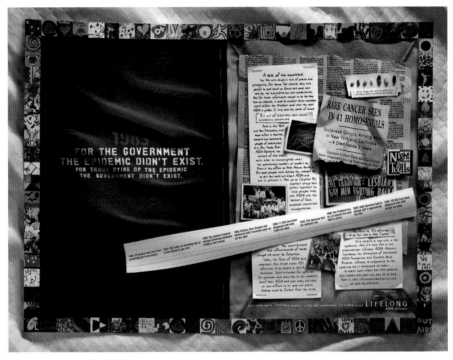

Fred Hammerquist Art Director: Randy, Gerda Designer: Todd Hofmeister Photographer: Todd Hofmeister Photographer: Daniel Langley Copywriter: Eric Gutierrez Traffic Director: Robyn Hallonquist Account Coordinator: Nancy Dickerson Client: Lifelong AIDS Alliance   Public Services 194, 195

'1983,' 'It's Been Proven' and 'We've All Got to Die' Agency: DDB Seattle Creative Director:

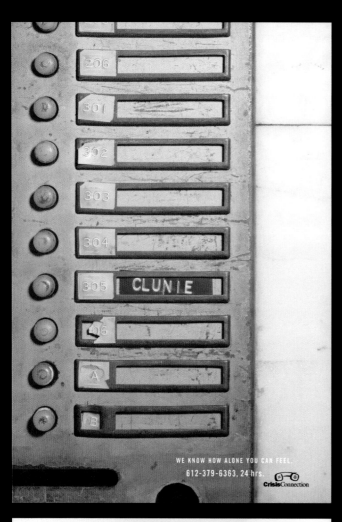

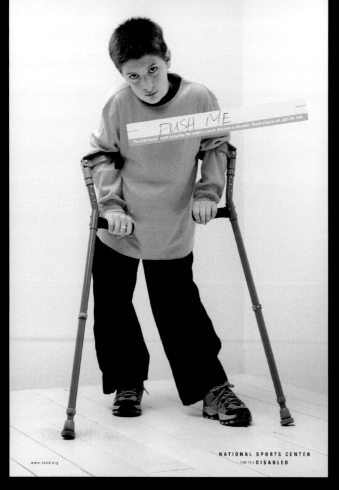

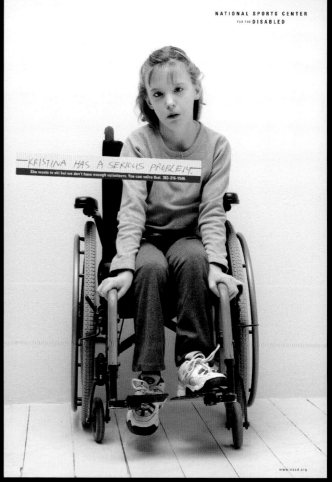

What kind of people take blind kids mountain climbing?

The same ones who take paraplegics sailing and amputees horseback riding.

NATIONAL SPORTS CENTER FOR THE DISABLED

To participate, volunteer, or help financially, visit www.nscd.org.

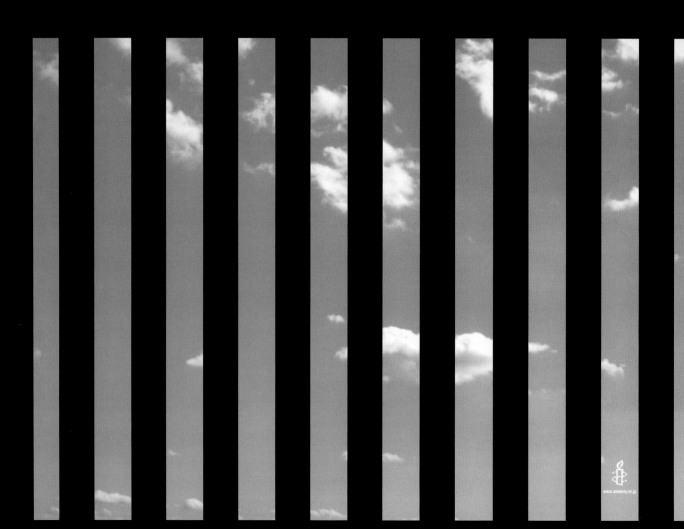

Public Services: 198,1999 Creative Director: Rich Silverstein Art Director: Rich Silverstein Designers: Shui Wong and Rich Silverstein Illustrators: R. Kenton Nelson, Michael Schwab and Craig Frazier Copywriter: Rich Silverstein Client: Golden Gate National Parks

'2001 Crissy Field Campaign' Agency: Goodby, Silverstein & Partners

"Look, it's only an abacus. It will help you learn to count. It can't hurt you. C'mon, you're just being silly. Don't you want to learn to count?" Parents can't help Autistic children, because they don't understand what they're going through. Friends and family can't help the parents, because they don't understand what they're going through. Autism effects over 2 million people in the UK. Yet most people can't even begin to understand it. The National Autistic Society. 08702 33 40 40.

Autism. The problem is understanding.

"Learning difficulties." "Behavioural disorder." "Mental illness." "Eccentric behaviour." "Attention Deficit Disorder." "Emotional problems." 40% of Autistic children wait more than 3 years for a clear diagnosis. Some are never diagnosed correctly. And until recently, some members of the medical profession even denied the very existence of Autism. Over 2 million people are effected by Autism in the UK. Yet most people can't even begin to understand it. The National Autistic Society. 08702 33 40 40.

Autism. The problem is understanding.

反贪艰难路，
不怕穿小鞋

反腐倡廉　振兴中华

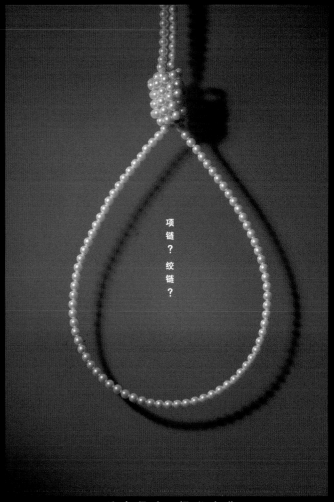

项
链
？
绞
链
？

反腐倡廉　振兴中华

(top) 'Fire' and 'Crossing' Agency: Walsh Trott Chick Smith Creative Director: Nick Wray Art Directors: Neil Croker and Steve Back Photographer: Leon Copywriters: Graham

Sherlock and Nick Wray Account Coordinator: Emily James Client: The National Autistic Society (bottom) 'Footprint' and 'Pearl Noose' Agency: TBWA/Lee/Davis Creative Director: Wendy Cheung Art Director: Helen Dou Designer: Anna

No bar or bolt can keep this attack out of the home. Asthma.

‡ AMERICAN LUNG ASSOCIATION®

Asthma fears nothing. It has already reached 26 million. To stop the epidemic, call 1-800-LUNG-USA or visit www.lungusa.org

ATTACK

No place is sacred. Asthma.

‡ AMERICAN LUNG ASSOCIATION

Asthma fears nothing. It has already reached 26 million. To stop the epidemic, call 1-800-LUNG-USA or visit www.lungusa.org

ATTACK

IT'S HER RIGHT TO SAY "NO."

IF YOU DON'T LISTEN, YOU'RE A RAPIST.

IT'S HER RIGHT TO SAY "NO."

IF YOU DON'T LISTEN, YOU'RE A RAPIST.

1-877-270 STOP

MINNESOTA'S TOBACCO HELPLINE

IF YOU SMOKE AROUND YOUR CHILDREN, THEY CAN INHALE THE EQUIVALENT OF 102 PACKS OF CIGARETTES BY AGE 5.

SECONDHAND SMOKE. STILL WANT TO BREATHE IT?

(top left) 'Bra' Agency: Clarity Coverdale Fury Creative Director: Jac Coverdale Art Director: Mark Sorensen Photographer: Curtis Johnson Copywriter: Terri Herber Client:

Public Services 202, 203

(top right) 'Button Fly' Agency: Clarity Coverdale Fury Creative Director: Jac Coverdale Art Director: Mark Sorensen Photographer: Curtis Johnson Copywriter: Troy Longie Client: MCASA (bottom left) 'Grim Reaper 2' Agency:

Pets can't fix themselves.

Friends of Animals
1-800-321-PETS
Affordable breeding control

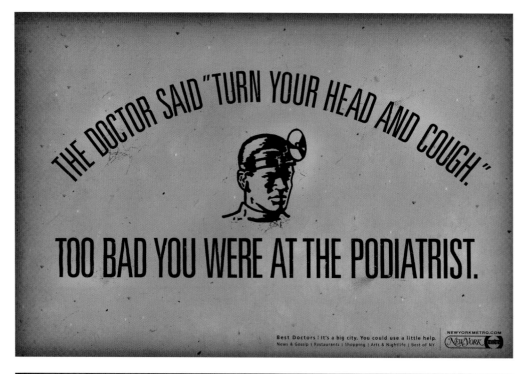

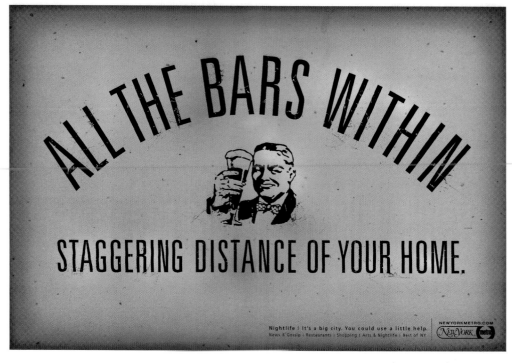

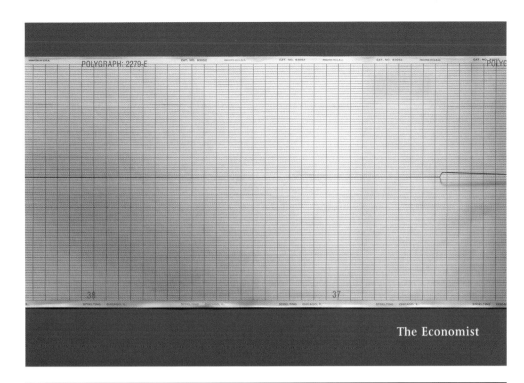

The Economist

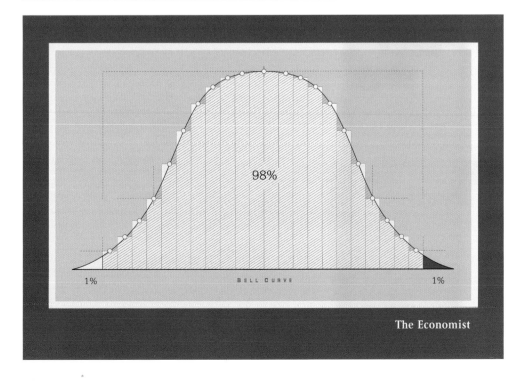

The Economist

'Polygraph,' 'Depth Gauge' and 'Bell Curve' Agency: Brand Architecture International Creative Director: Marty Weiss Art Director: Ralph Watson Photographer: Hans Gissinger Copywriter: Ken Marcus Client: The Economist   Publishing 206,207

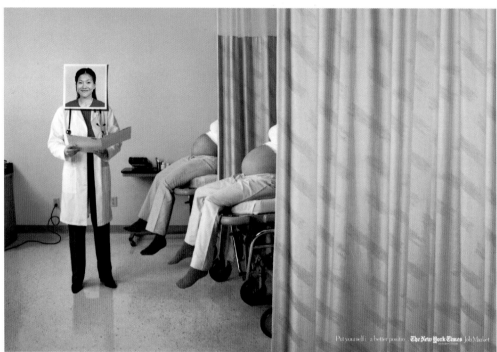

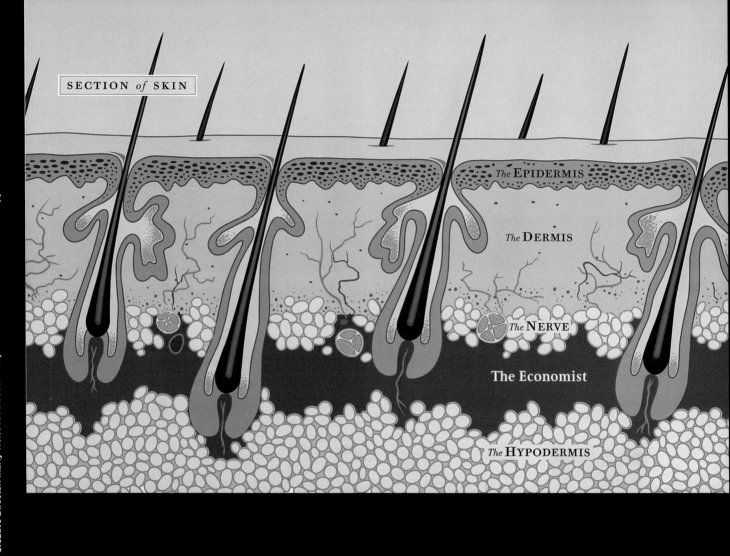

SECTION *of* SKIN

The EPIDERMIS

The DERMIS

The NERVE

The Economist

The HYPODERMIS

the *corcoran* group
Exceptional Real Estate

the *corcoran* group
Exceptional Real Estate

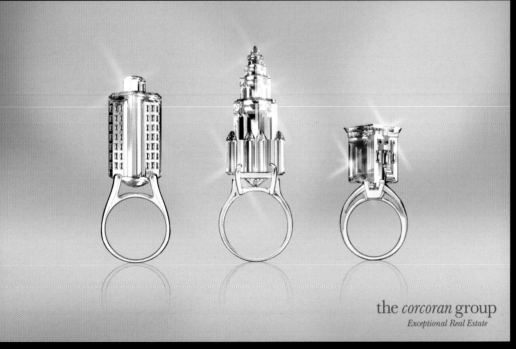

the *corcoran* group
Exceptional Real Estate

Creative Director: Guy Seese Art Directors: Guy Seese and James Dawson-Hollis Photographer: Steve Hellerstein Copywriter: Craig Miller Digital Illustrator: Backbone NYC Account Coordinator: Robin Hafitz Client: The Corcoran Group   Publishing 210.21

'Chocolate,' 'Sushi' and 'Rings' Agency: Mad Dogs and Englishmen

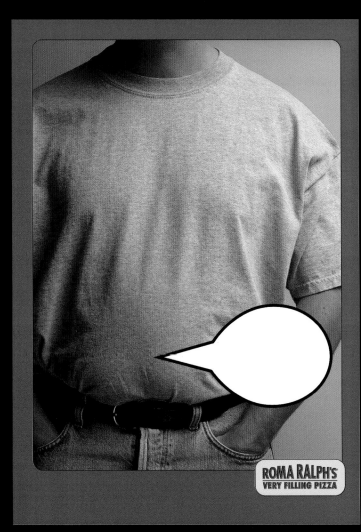

ROMA RALPH'S
VERY FILLING PIZZA

SEE THE SUPERBOWL TEX-MEX STYLE

'Drunk' Agency: Jung von Matt/Limmat AG Creative Directors: Daniel Meier and Alexander Jaggy Art Director: Simon Stamb Designer: Martin Friedlin Photographer: Stefan Minder Client: FC St. Pauli Bar

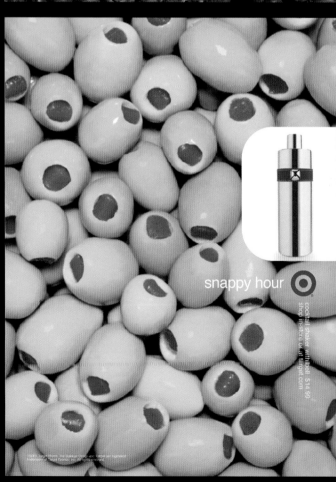

Eldorado Look Edition

Spring-Summer Collection

September, 25, 2001

Eldorado Look Edition

Spring-Summer Collection

September, 25, 2001

Eldorado Look Edition

Spring-Summer Collection

September, 25, 2001

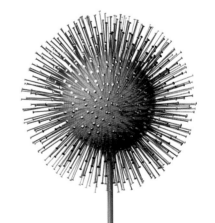

Eldorado Look Edition

Spring-Summer Collection

September, 25, 2001

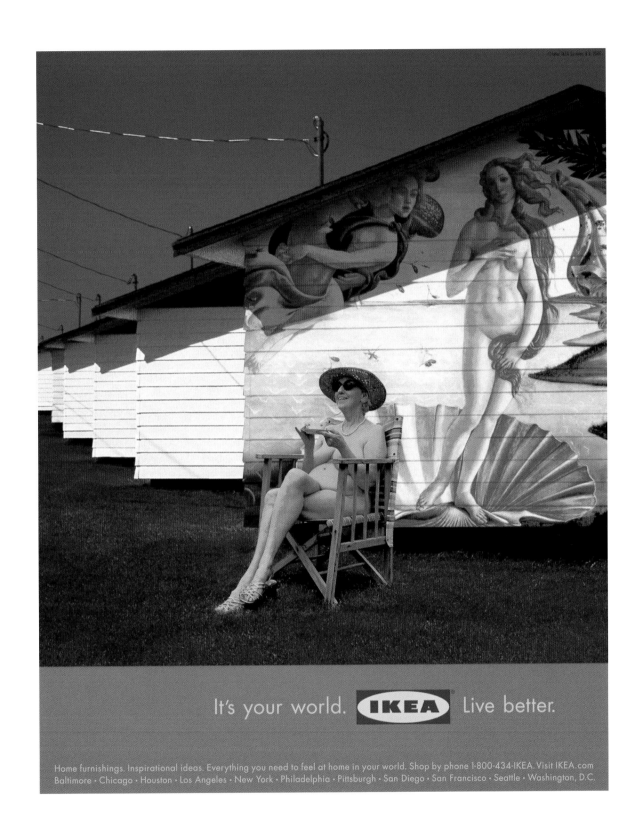

It's your world. **IKEA** Live better.

Home furnishings. Inspirational ideas. Everything you need to feel at home in your world. Shop by phone 1-800-434-IKEA. Visit IKEA.com
Baltimore · Chicago · Houston · Los Angeles · New York · Philadelphia · Pittsburgh · San Diego · San Francisco · Seattle · Washington, D.C.

'Venus' Agency: Carmichael Lynch Creative Director: Jud Smith Art Director: Penny Duerr Copywriter: Katie Franzen Client: Ikea

Pretension doesn't sit well here.

ANTÈKS

Outfitters of home furnishings and accessories.

Dallas · Houston · Atlanta · Kansas City · Los Angeles · San Antonio · Plano

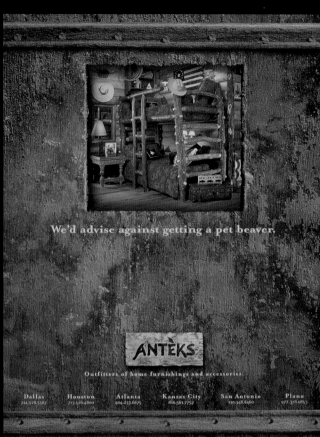

We'd advise against getting a pet beaver.

ANTÈKS

Outfitters of home furnishings and accessories.

Dallas · Houston · Atlanta · Kansas City · San Antonio · Plano

Unstained
Unpainted. Unvarnished. Uninhibited.

STARRING: CHERRY VARNISH and BUCK NAKED

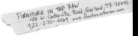

"Honey, close the door before
the ottoman gets out."

ANTÈKS

Outfitters of home furnishings and accessories.

Dallas	Houston	Atlanta	Kansas City	San Antonio	Plano
214.528.5567	713.526.4800	404.233.6675	816.561.7757	210.348.6460	972.378.0853

Finds it perfectly natural
to have sex with sheep.

Get to know the outdoors better.

513 North 36th Seattle 206.545.8810 11-6 7 Days

Used by great chefs.

Used by dead chefs.

Get to know the outdoors better.

513 North 36th Seattle 206.545.8810 11-6 7 Days

Butterflies have a lifespan
of three months.

Month 1: born

Month 2: joins gang

Month 3: dies

Get to know the outdoors better.

513 North 36th Seattle 206.545.8810 11-6 7 Days

THIS IS A CAMOUFLAGE PRINT DRESS BY FERRE. YOU'LL NEVER FIND IT.

ETERNIA

Exclusive designer clothes and accessories for women. From Fendi to Ferre. Tommy Hilfiger to Thierry Mugler. You'll find them at Eternia, Premsons Bazaar, Breach Candy. If you're lucky. Here today. Gone tomorrow.

IF YOU LIKE THIS DOLCE & GABBANA SUIT SO MUCH, KEEP STARING AT IT. THAT'S ALL YOU CAN DO NOW THAT RHEA SEN'S BOUGHT IT.

ETERNIA

Exclusive designer clothes and accessories for women. From DKNY to D & G. Fendi to Ferre. At Eternia, Premsons Bazaar, Breach Candy. Hurry, they'll be gone in the wink of an eye. Here today. Gone tomorrow.

YESTERDAY, THIS WAS THE VERSACE COLLECTION AT ETERNIA, BREACH CANDY. TODAY, IT IS THE SOHAYA COLLECTION AT CITADEL, NAPEAN ROAD.

ETERNIA

Exclusive designer clothes and accessories for men and women. From Versace to Valentino. Krizia to Kenzo. Now at Eternia, Premsons Bazaar, Breach Candy. Tomorrow, they could be gone. Here today. Gone tomorrow.

You won't need **Prozac.**

Your husband won't need **Viagra.**

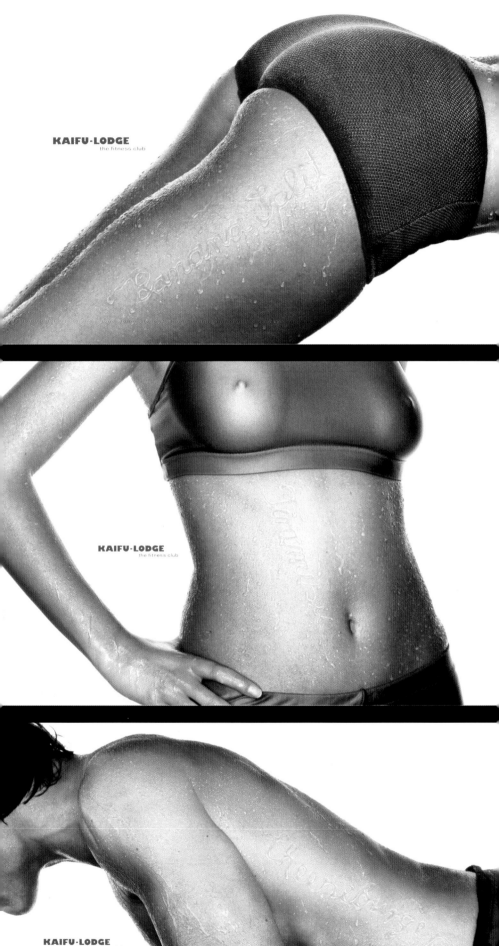

KAIFU·LODGE
the fitness club

KAIFU·LODGE
the fitness club

KAIFU·LODGE
the fitness club

How to best exploit the fact big fish still eat little fish.

★ **Show them what they're used to eating.** A trophy fish has been living in the same environment for as long as it took to become a trophy. And while it might be fooled by something different when in an aggressive mood, it's most comfortable eating whatever forage is native to the area. When it comes to matching the forage, no one offers more choices than Rapala. Which is why fish will take a carefully selected Rapala as unthinkingly as you'd amble over to your fridge and grab a slice of leftover pizza.

★ **Don't know the exact forage?** Virtually any fishable water hosts baitfish with the stout, round shape reminiscent of perch, shad and shiners. These are the fish more big fish eat, and the Rapala Shad Rap® could be their clone. In fact, when the Shad Rap was first introduced, it fooled fish so well with its distinct silhouette and tight, wounded-minnow wobble, tackle shops rented them for $20 a day. Today the venerable Shad Rap comes in all sizes, colors and running depths, and is available jointed, suspending or rattling, to match any condition and mood.

★ **Bump the stump.** Fishing rule #1: Fish relate to structure. This can mean rocks, stumps, docks, pilings, points, humps, vegetation or any other irregularity. Once you've located such an ambush point, tie on a Fat Rap® and literally bounce the lure off of it. Fish will see the more erratic bumping, swimming action as an aggressively feeding minnow, and an easy mark. Or choose one of Fat Rap's three highly detailed crawdad patterns, and it's a tasty crawfish blindly scrambling from an unseen predator. And into the jaws of Mr. Big.

★ **How to get on top of fish.** After a sudden cold snap or during the hot, dog days of August, fish will set up along the deeper structure. Conversely, spring, early morning or late evening may find them aggressively hitting topwater, and this is when the Rapala Skitter Pop™ is in its glory. Give it a steady retrieve while pumping the rod tip to imitate a fleeing baitfish. Or pop it with a sharp jerk, then let it stop, like a leopard frog resting on the soon-to-be-shattered surface.

★ **Big fish, small appetite?** When the water's murky or after a fast-moving cold front, the big predators need to be reminded of their role in life. That's when the new Tail Dancer™ wades in to lubricate those firmly locked jaws. By combining the classic action of a balsa wood Rapala with a more pronounced, 'come hither' tail wobble and built-in rattle, it'll never have problems finding dance partners.

★ **The first lure to truly fool fish.** Long and narrow in profile, the Original Floater™ resembles soft-finned baitfish like cisco and suckers, and is easily the most versatile lure in your arsenal. Twitch it on top. Slow retrieve it to just bulge the surface. Cast normally over weeds. Troll it shallow, or at further depths simply by adding weight. It's the lure that gave birth to the legendary wounded-minnow action, which is still hand-tuned and tank-tested into each and every Rapala. And as long as big fish still eat the little ones, we'll continue to do so.

Rapala

Cast like a pro. Consult wife before actually quitting day job.
Limited-edition Longcast Minnow™ One lure for every 185 anglers. Don't be left short.

Rapala

Fishing without one is called boating.
The new rattling, suspending Jointed Shad Rap® There goes your relaxing day on the lake.

Rapala

How to organize a fish search party.

★ **They're either shallow, deep or somewhere in between.** If there's one thing successful fishermen know, it's this: Before you can get a fish to bite a lure, you must first put a lure in front of a fish. In other words, fish where the fish are. They've got to be somewhere. You just have to get in front of them. Right in the strike zone. Do it consistently, and it's just a matter of time before you're ripping lips at a rate that could get you your own fishing show.

★ **How to work the legendary Shad Raps like a fine-toothed comb.** Take any piece of fishing structure on any good water in the world, and one thing holds true: There are always fish relating to it. They may be on top, chomping in the shallows. Hiding in ambush along the deep weed edge. Laying low in the rocks at the base of the drop-off. Or out in nearby open water feeding on suspended baitfish. The simple fact is, they're there. And there is no better way to get at them than by pressing a full lineup of Shad Raps into service. By starting with the Shallow Shad Rap® and working your way up through the sizes of the others as you move deeper (the bigger the Shad Rap, the deeper it runs), you can put a lure right in the strike zone wherever the fish are, top to bottom.

Work each level thoroughly, methodically, then, once you make contact, zero in. Repeat the pattern. And let the fishing bonanza begin.

★ **In this search, the Shad Rap gets destroyed.** No other lure has provoked more bone-jarring strikes than the Shad Rap. From its introduction, when bait shops were renting them out for as much as $20 a day, until now, its renown has only grown. The secret is in the delicate wounded-minnow wobble that only a lure made from balsa wood, then carefully hand-tuned and tank-tested, can provide. The subtle Rapala action is different than any other lure and, as time has proven, far superior to lures made from lesser materials in hastier ways. With an arsenal of Shad Raps, you can match your presentation precisely to the fish's mood. The original Shad Rap® and Shallow Shad Rap® offer the purest action you can put in the water. In clear water, or on days when only the most subtle action will do, it's the one. When fish need a little more, the Shad Rap® RS adds a rattle. It will also snapd in the fish's face, begging for a collision. On days when you need to throw them a curve, try the Jointed Shad Rap® It's wider, noisier wobble can be just what the lunker ordered.

★ **More fish. Bigger fish. Any questions?** If you work the Shad Raps to their full potential, you will reap hefty rewards. The fact is, Rapala lures currently hold more world records than any other lure. Why not spend some time of your own out there, searching high and low for the next one?

Rapala

WE'LL TAKE CARE OF THE VENTILATION. YOU TAKE CARE OF THE WHIMPERING AND INTENSE DESIRE TO BE HELD.

Besides having vertical rear vents, our patented push-to-fit Brain Trust helmets just plain fit better. Whether you're out all day riding (or bathing) this tends to come in handy. The whimpering, well, that's your problem.

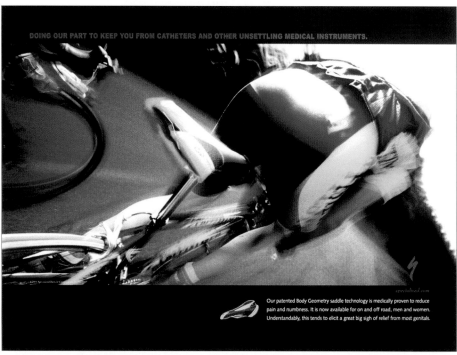

DOING OUR PART TO KEEP YOU FROM CATHETERS AND OTHER UNSETTLING MEDICAL INSTRUMENTS.

Our patented Body Geometry saddle technology is medically proven to reduce pain and numbness. It is now available for on and off road, men and women. Understandably, this tends to elicit a great big sigh of relief from most genitals.

NOTHING LIKE SPENDING THE DAY OUT OF FOCUS.

We've developed shoes that actually enable you to pedal faster. Thanks to our patent pending Body Geometry technology (and tireless scientists) your legs no longer have to be solely responsible for sending you into pass/blur mode.

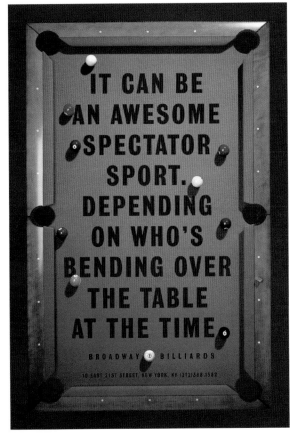
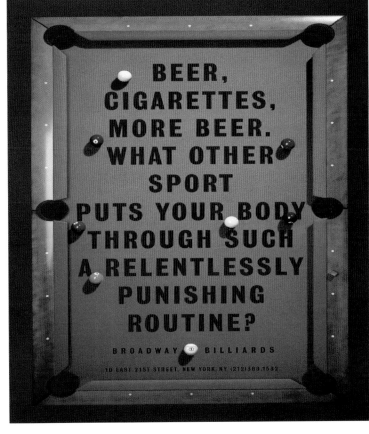

Agency: Bozell New York Creative Director: Tony Granger Art Director: Steve Mitsch Photographer: Andy Spreitzer Copywriters: Richard Wallace and David Nobay Group Creative Director: David Nobay Client: Broadway Billiards

'Spectator Sport' and 'Punishing Routine'

Razor-sharp handling.

VOLANT

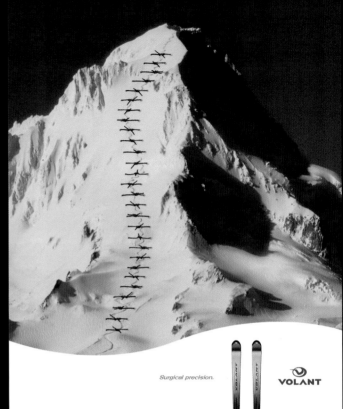

Surgical precision.

VOLANT

The Old Man and the Sea. Captains Courageous. Huckleberry Finn.

We've yet to read a great adventure novel about a fiberglass cigarette boat.

Wind, water, wood, canvas. These are the elements of some of life's greatest stories. Come spend the day in a classic wooden boat. Bring pen and ink. 1010 Valley Street, Seattle, WA 98109, 206.382.2628, cwb.org.

The Center For Wooden Boats

(this spread) Agency: Bates Yomiko Creative Director: Marcus Woolcott Art Directors: Marcus Woolcott and Kiyotaka Kobayashi Designer: Marcus Woolcott Photographers: Marcus Woolcott and Jeff Browns Copywriter: Craig McDean and Jeff Browns Copywriter: Marcus Woolcott Client: Lucky Strike Japan

Coordinator: Leena Silfverberg Client: Finnish Tourist Board

(this spread) 'Snow Globe' and 'Santa Claus' Agency: TBWA/PHS Creative Directors: Zoubida Benkhellat and Markku Ronkko Art Director: Zoubida Benkhellat Illustrators: Tommi Vallisto and Ilkka Juoperi Copywriter: Markku Ronkko Planner: Anna Mollanen Account

WHITE CHRISTMAS GUARANTEED.

www.GoNowFinland.com

WHITE CHRISTMAS GUARANTEED. ✚ *Finland*
www.GoNowFinland.com

'Office' and 'Deadline' Agency: Loeffler Ketchum Mountjoy Creative Director: Jim Mountjoy Art Director: Doug Pedersen Photographers: Olaf Veltman and Pat Staub (left); Harry DeZitter (right) Copywriter: Curtis Smith Account Coordinators: John Ketchum and Dawn

Loeffler Ketchum Mountjoy Creative Director: Jim Mountjoy Art Director: Doug Pedersen Photographer: Stuart Hall Copywriter: Curtis Smith Account Coordinators: John Ketchum and Dawn Coleman Client: North Carolina Travel & Tourism   Travel 238, 239

'While You Were Out,' 'Relaxation Clinic' and 'Drive In' Agency:

THE LAND IS UNSPOILED. YOU, HOWEVER, WON'T BE.

It is difficult to say which state you will reach first. That of Alaska? Or of complete and utter relaxation. Whichever it may be,

one thing is certain, however. You will be well-rested to explore the dramatic, awe-inspiring interior

Celebrity Cruises®

of America's last virgin frontier. Call 1-800-CELEBRITY or peruse further at celebritycruises.com

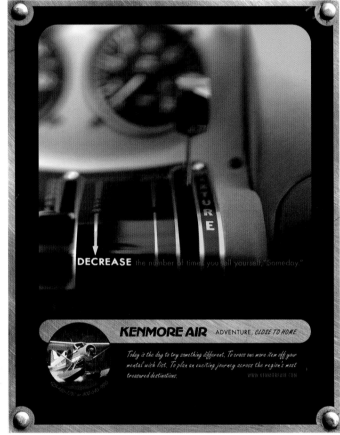

German Rail **DB**

Please don't fold away your tables, don't bring your seats to the upright position, don't fasten your seatbelts, and don't switch off your electronic devices. Get on board – at a station near you, see your local travel agent or visit www.bahn.de

German Rail **DB**

When will trains be on time? When will there be train fares we can understand? When will trains and stations be more up-to-date? When was the last time you travelled by train? Get on board – at a station near you, see your local travel agent or visit www.bahn.de

German Rail **DB**

One should forbid trees from falling onto tracks, discourage lovers' long goodbyes and make elderly people run when compelled to. But we won't do any of this. Get on board – at a station near you, see your local German Rail licensed travel agent or visit www.bahn.de

Agency: Jung von Matt/Fleet Creative Directors: Constantin Kaloff and Ove Gley Art Director: Andreas Ruthermann Photographers: Max Galli and Michael Schnabel Copywriters: Daniel Frericks and Candan Sasmaz Client: Deutsche Bahn AG

The city of love.
A thousand-year-old theater. Two seats.
Tonight's performance: sunset.

If true love is indeed timeless, there may well be no better place on earth to find it than Aphrodisias. Will you find it at the temple of Aphrodite herself? Or at the awesome spectacle of the 30,000-seat stadium, one of the best-preserved in the Greco-Roman world? Regardless, love, like culture and history, is at home in Turkey. Could it be because it has been growing wild here for so many thousands of years? Call 1-877-FOR-TURKEY or visit www.tourismturkey.org

Remember the stories of
mystical places and foreign lands
you heard as a child?
They're true.

Have your eyes deceived you or did a person just disappear into a distant rock? Welcome to the fairy chimneys of Cappadocia. Through ancient passageways, you may enter one of the underground dwellings scattered throughout this land. Or one of the churches or cities carved from the soft, volcanic rock. Some are still inhabited. And more are being found. What wonders will you discover? Call 1-877-FOR-TURKEY or visit www.tourismturkey.org

Mark Antony once gave
this stretch of coast to his beloved Cleopatra.
Who will you give it to?

A tremendous teal-blue jewel. This Aegean coastline has seen centuries of civilizations rise, fall, war, trade, disappear and reappear. It has witnessed the birth of great religions. It has watched culture, art, government and literature flourish. It has seen pirates hide treasure. And it has watched many come to seek its beauty and wonder at its depths. Will you be one? Learn more. Call 1-877-FOR-TURKEY or visit www.tourismturkey.org

To understand someone, walk in their footsteps.
In the case of
Alexander the Great,
follow this path.

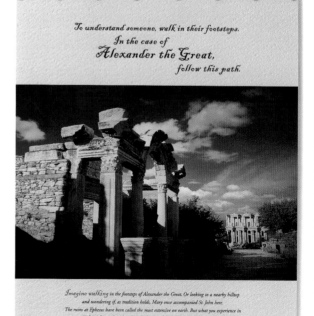

Imagine walking in the footsteps of Alexander the Great. Or looking to a nearby hilltop and wondering if, as tradition holds, Mary once accompanied St. John here. The ruins at Ephesus have been called the most extensive on earth. But what you experience in Turkey is larger than this place, the beauty of the land, the teal-blue Aegean. It is history and culture, East and West, old and new. And it is unlike anything you have ever seen. Learn more. Call 1-877-FOR-TURKEY or visit www.tourismturkey.org

Just an hour's drive from Chennai, spread across a pristine white beach, lies an international resort:
Sea-facing cottages and rooms. Blue waters. Fresh seafood. No visas. Call (04114) 72304 or visit www.tajhotels.com

Fisherman's Cove *Chennai*

Just an hour's drive from Chennai, spread across a pristine white beach, lies an international resort:
Sea-facing cottages and rooms. Blue waters. Fresh seafood. No visas. Call (04114) 72304 or visit www.tajhotels.com

Fisherman's Cove *Chennai*

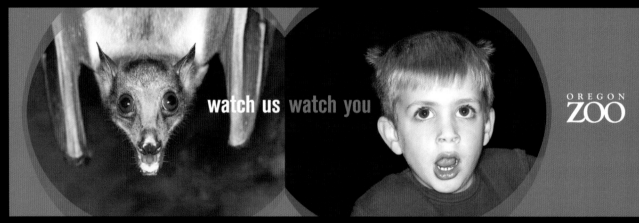

'Bird Lady' Agency: Cole & Weber/Red Cell Creative Director: Guy Seese Art Directors: Kathy Vinceri and Guy Seese Photographer: Lars Topelmann Copywriter: Lars Topelmann Copywriter: Jim Elliott Account Coordinator: Rebecca Armstrong Digital Artist: Sean

CreativeDirectorsArtDirectorsDesigners

PhotographersIllustrators

Copywriters

Agencies

Clients

Directory of Advertising Agencies

www.collemcvoy.com

Crispin Porter + Bogusky
2699 South Bayshore Drive
Miami, FL 33133
Tel: 1 305 859 2070
Fax: 1 305 854 3419
www.cpbgroup.com

D'Adda
Via Lanzone 4
Milan, Italy 20121
Tel: 39 02 880071
Fax: 39 02 88007223

David Stone Copywriter
2810 West 10th Avenue, #202
Denver, CO 80210
Tel: 1 303 715 1884

DDB Berlin
Neue Schönhauser Strasse 3-5
Berlin, Germany 10178
Tel: 030 240 840
Fax: 030 240 84 300
www.bln.ddbn.de

DDB Seattle
1008 Western Avenue, Suite 601
Seattle, WA 98104
Tel: 1 206 326 5105
Fax: 1 206 447 1201
www.sea.ddb.com

DeVito/Verdi
100 Avenue of the Americas
New York, NY 10013
Tel: 1 212 431 4694
Fax: 1 212 431 4940

DGWB
217 North Main Street, #200
Santa Ana, CA 92701
Tel: 1 714 881 2300
Fax: 1 714 881 2444
www.dgwb.com

Edson, FCB
Rva Bramcamp, No 40, 7th Floor
Lisbon, Portugal 1250 050
Tel: 352 21381 1200
Fax: 352 21384 1700
www.fcb.pt

EURO RSCG McConnaughty Tatham
36 East Grand Avenue
Chicago, IL 60611
Tel: 1 312 337 4400
Fax: 1 312 33712316

FCB Seattle
1011 Western Avenue Suite 1000
Seattle, WA 98104
Tel: 1 206 223 6464
Fax: 1 206 223 2765
www.seattle.fcb.com

FCB Southern California
17600 Gilette
Irvine, CA
Tel: 1 949 567 9166
Fax: 1 949 567 9465
www.socal.fcb.com

Fischer América
Av. Prof. Alceu Maynard Araújo, 698
São Paulo, Brazil 04726-160
Tel: 55 11 5641 1411
Fax: 55 11 5641 2343
www.fischeramerica.com.br

GDS Europe SW
Corso Monforte, 16
Milano, Italy 20122
Tel: 61 91 910 1000
Fax: 61 91 910 1009
www.gdsglobal.com

Goodby, Silverstein & Partners
720 California Street
San Francisco, CA 94108
Tel: 1 415 676 4597
Fax: 1 415 392 4920
www.gspsf.com

Grey Worldwide (I) PVT, Ltd.
Block 2-D, 3rd Floor, Phoenix Estate, 462
Tulsi Pipe Road
Mumbai, MaharashtraIndia 400 013
Tel: 91 22 460 6510
Fax: 91 22 4939355
www.greyindia.com

GSD&M Advertising
828 West 6th Street
Austin, TX 78703
Tel: 1 512 242 5800
Fax: 1 512 242 8800
www.gsdm.com

Henderson Advertising
60 Pointe Circle
Greenville, SC 29615
Tel: 1 864 271 6000
Fax: 1 864 298 1280
www.hendersonadv.com

Heye
Ottobrunner Strasse 28
Unterhaching, Germany 82008
Tel: 49 89 66532 340
Fax: 49 89 66532 380
www.heye.de

Hill Holliday
345 Hudson Street
New York, NY 10014
Tel: 1 212 830 7500
Fax: 1 212 830 7600
www.hhanyo.com

HSR Business to Business
300 East Business Way, Suite 500
Cincinnati, OH 45241
Tel: 1 513 671 3811
Fax: 1 513 671 8163
www.hsrb2b.com

Impiric Singapore
300 Beach Road, #33-00
Singapore 199555
Tel: 65 295 0975
Fax: 65 296 8352

Jung von Matt/Alster GmbH
Glashuettenstrasse 79
Hamburg, Germany 20357
Tel: 49 40 4321 1372
Fax: 49 40 4321 1214
www.jvm.de

Jung von Matt/Limmat AG
Wolfbachstrasse 19
Zurich, Switzerland CH-8032
Tel: 41 1254 6600
Fax: 41 1254 6601
www.jvm.ch

Karacters Design Group
1600-777 Hornby Street
Vancouver, British Columbia
Canada V6Z2T3
Tel: 1 604 640 4327
Fax: 1 604 608 4452
www.karacters.com

Kelliher Samets Volk
212 Battery Street
Burlington, MA 02113
Tel: 1 802 862 8261
Fax: 1 802 863 4724

Kilmer & Kilmer
125 Truman Northeast Suite 200
Albuquerque, NM 87108
Tel: 1 505 260 1175
Fax: 1 505 260 1155
www.kilmer2.com

Klaus E. Kuster Webeagentur
Alexanderstrasse 65
Frankfurt, Germany 60489
Tel: 49 6 9978 8030
Fax: 49 6 9978 80322
www.kek.de

Lietzee Nut
539 West End Avenue
New York, NY 10024
Tel: 1 212 724 3847

Loeffler Ketchum Mountjoy
2101 Rexford Road, Suite 200E
Charlotte, NC 28211
Tel: 1 704 364 8969
Fax: 1 704 364 8470
www.lkmads.com

Lowe
One Dag Hammarskjold Plaza, 41st Floor
New York, NY 10017-2203
Tel: 1 212 605 8192
Fax: 1 212 605 4709
www.loweworldwide.com

Lowe Bangkok
195, 27-28th Floor, Empire Tower Building,
South Sathorn Road, Yannawa, Sathorn
Bangkok, Thailand 10120
Tel: 662 670 1000
Fax: 662 670 1062
www.loweworldwide.com

Lunar Design
541 Eighth Street
San Francisco, CA 94103
Tel: 1 415 252 4388
Fax: 1 415 252 4389
www.lunar.com

Mad Dogs and Englishmen
126 5th Avenue, 12th Floor
New York, NY 10011
Tel: 1 212 675 6116
Fax: 1 212 675 0340
www.maddogsandenglishmen.com

Malcolm Moore
Elsley Court, 20-22 Great Titchfield Street
London, United Kindom W1W8BE
Tel: 44 20 7908 7510
Fax: 44 20 7908 7511

Mangos
10 Great Valley Parkway, Suite 160
Malvern, PA 19355-1316
Tel: 1 610 296 2555
Fax: 1 610 640 9291
www.mangosinc.com

Martin/Williams, Inc.
60 South 6th Street, Suite 2800
Minneapolis, MN 55402
Tel: 1 612 342 9844
Fax: 1 612 342 4375
www.martinwilliams.com

McCann -Erickson
135 Main Street
San Francisco, CA 94105
Tel: 1 415 348 5100
Fax: 1 415 357 1088
www.mccannsf.com

McCann-Erickson Guangming Limited
23/F, Sunning Plaza, 10 Hysan Avenue
Causeway Bay, Hong KongChina
Tel: 852 2808 7888
Fax: 852 2890 5545

McGarrah/Jessee
205 Brazos Street
Austin, TX 78701
Tel: 1 512 225 2000
Fax: 1 512 225 2020
www.mc-j.com

Mullen
38 Essex Street
Wenham, MA 01984
Tel: 1 978 468 8734
Fax: 1 978 468 1133
www.mullen.com

Muller & Company
4739 Belleview
Kansas City, MO 64112
Tel: 1 816 531 1992
Fax: 1 816 531 6692
www.mullerco.com

Olson & Company
1625 Hennepin Avenue
Minneapolis, MN 55403
Tel: 1 612 215 9800
Fax: 1 612 215 9801
www.oco.com

Peterson Milla Hooks
1315 Harmon Place
Minneapolis, MN 55402
Tel: 1 612 304 0178
Fax: 1 612 304 5104

Publicis & Hal Riney
2001 The Embarcadero
San Francisco, CA 94133
Tel: 1 415 293 2447
Fax: 1 415 293 2620
www.hrp.com

Publicis in Midamerica
224 South Michigan Avenue
Chicago, IL 60604
Tel: 1 312 697 5747
Fax: 1 312 697 5770
www.publicis-usa.com

Publicis Werbeagentur GmbH
Walther-von-Cronberg-Platz 6
Frankfurt, Germany 60594
Tel: 49 69 15402 441
Fax: 49 69 15402 370
www.publicis-frankfurt.de

Rainey Kelly Campbell Roalfe/Young &
Rubicam
Greater London House, Hempstead Road
London, United Kingdom NW1 7QP
Tel: 44 20 7611 6000
www.yr.com

Rethinking Group
Wilemstraat 1l
Eindhoven, The Netherlands 5611HA
Tel: 31 40 24 33767
Fax: 31 40 26 33768

Robaire & Hogshead
905 Electric Avenue, Loft C
Venice, CA 90291
Tel: 1 310 452 6222
Fax: 1 310 452 4664
www.rohog.com

Rodgers Townsend
1310 Papin
St. Louis, MO 63103
Tel: 1 314 436 9960
Fax: 1 314 436 9961
www.rodgerstownsend.com

RTS Rieger Team
Bunsenstrasse 7-9
Leinfelden-Ech., Germany 70771
Tel: 49 711 975 2112
Fax: 49 711 975 2180
www.rts-riegerteam.de

Rubin Postaer and Associates
1333 Second Street
Santa Monica, CA 90401
Tel: 1 310 917 2434
Fax: 1 310 656 4709
www.rpa.com

Saatchi & Saatchi India
Sitram Mills com. Delisle Road
Mumbai, India 400011
Tel: 9122 300 0301
Fax: 9122 300 0202
www.saatchiindia.com

Sandstrom Design
808 Southwest Third Avenue, #610
Portland, OR 97204
Tel: 1 503 248 9466
Fax: 1 503 227 5035
www.sandstromdesign.com

Signland
36, Av. Heri Matisse
Nice, France 06200
Tel: 33 04 93 72 11 30
Fax: 33 04 93 72 11 40
www.signland.com

Slow-motion
213 East 30th Street No. 2E
Kansas City, MO 64108
Tel: 1 816 756 1206

Sony Music Entertainment
550 Madison Avenue
New York, NY 10022
Tel: 1 212 833 5881
www.sonymusic.com

Stone and Walker
2126 South Franklin Street
Denver, CO 80210
Tel: 1 303 715 1884

Sukle Advertising
2430 West 32nd Avenue
Denver, CO 80211
Tel: 1 303 964 9100
Fax: 1 303 964 9663
www.sukle.com

Taxi
495 Wellington St. W.
Toronto, Ontario
Canada M5VIE9
Tel: 1 416 979 4402
Fax: 1 416 979 7626
www.taxi.ca

TBWA/Lee/Davis
29/F, Hong Kong Plaza, South Tower, 283
Huaihai Zhong
Shanghai, China 200201
Tel: 862163906798
Fax: 862163906279
www.tbwa-sh.com

TBWA/PHS
Tehtaankatu 1a
Helsinki, Finland FIN00140
Tel: 358 9 171 711
Fax: 358 9 171 811
www.phs.fi

The Ant Farm
910 North Sycamore Avenue
Los Angeles, CA 90038
Tel: 1 323 850 0700
Fax: 1 323 850 0777

The Richards Group
8750 North Central Expressway, #1200
Dallas, TX 75231
Tel: 1 214 891 2820
Fax: 1 214 891 2911
www.richards.com

Toth Brand Imaging
30 Monument Square
Concord, MA 01742
Tel: 1 978 369 3917
Fax: 1 978 369 6774
www.toth.com

Tribe
180 Cyprus Avenue
Tampa, FL 33606
Tel: 1 813 202 1227
Fax: 1 813 222 0849
www.tribeads.com

Walsh Trott Chick Smith
Holden House, 57 Rathbone Place
London, United Kingdom W1TJ1U
Tel: 44 20 7907 1200
Fax: 44 20 7907 1201
www.wtcs.co.uk

Westwayne
1170 Peachtree Street, 15th Floor
Atlanta, GA 30309
Tel: 1 404 347 8868
www.westwayne.com

Wieden + Kennedy, Amsterdam
Keizersgracht 125-127
Amsterdam, The Netherlands 1015 CJ
Tel: 31 20 7126500
Fax: 31 20 7216699
www.wk.com

Wongdoody/Seattle
216 First Avenue South, Suite 480
Seattle, WA 98104
Tel: 1 206 624 5325
Fax: 1 206 624 2369
www.wongdoody.com

Young and Laramore
310 East Vermont Street
Indianapolis, IN 46204
Tel: 1 317 264 8000
Fax: 1 317 264 8001
www.youngandlaramore.com

Young & Rubicam Brasil
Av. Brigadeiro Faria Lima, 1355 - 19th Floor
São Paulo, Brasil 01452002
Tel: 55 11 3097 7731
Fax: 55 11 3097 7709
www.yr.com

Young & Rubicam, New York
285 Madison Avenue
New York, NY 10017
Tel: 1 212 210 4552

Young & Rubicam Vancouver
1100 Melville Street
Vancouver, British Columbia
Canada V6E 4A6
Tel: 1 604 689 3895